Better Homes and Gardens®

WOOD™

HOLIDAY GIFTS

YOU CAN MAKE

━━━━━ **WE CARE!** ━━━━━

All of us at Meredith® Books are dedicated to giving you the
information and ideas you need to create beautiful and useful
woodworking projects. We guarantee your satisfaction with this
book for as long as you own it. We also welcome your comments
and suggestions. Please write us at Meredith® Books, BB-117,
1716 Locust St., Des Moines, IA 50309-3400.

A **WOOD**™ **BOOK**
Published by Meredith® Books

MEREDITH® BOOKS
President, Book Group: Joseph J. Ward
Vice President and Editorial Director: Elizabeth P. Rice
Executive Editor: Connie Schrader
Art Director: Ernest Shelton
Prepress Production Manager: Randall Yontz

WOOD® MAGAZINE
President, Magazine Group: William T. Kerr
Editor: Larry Clayton

HOLIDAY GIFTS YOU CAN MAKE
Produced by Roundtable Press, Inc.
Directors: Susan E. Meyer, Marsha Melnick
Senior Editor: Marisa Bulzone
Managing Editor: Ross L. Horowitz
Graphic Designer: Leah Lococo
Design Assistant: Leslie Goldman
Art Assistant: Marianna Canelo Francis
Copy Assistant: Amy Handy

For Meredith® Books
Editorial Project Manager/Assistant Art Director: Tom Wegner
Contributing How-To Editors: Marlen Kemmet,
    Beverly Rivers, Charles E. Sommers
Contributing Tool Editor: Larry Johnston
Contributing Outline Editor: David A. Kirchner

Special thanks to Khristy Benoit

On the front cover: Holiday Candle Holder, pages 30–31
On the back cover (clockwise from top left): Heirloom Tree
    Ornaments, pages 9–10; Hardwood Bookends, pages
    58–59; Handwoven What-Not Basket, pages 76–79

YULETIDE ORNAMENTS AND DECORATIONS

Your home and hearth will be decked out in true holiday style with this group of projects. Perfect for keeping or giving, these decorations will warm hearts for many seasons to come.

HARK, THE HERALD CRITTERS SING!

They're not the Kingston Trio, but these carolers will be a howling success when you prop them up in your front yard. Painting got you worried? No problem—it's as simple as a coloring book, only bigger.

Cut out the plywood and get primed for some fun

1. Transfer the pattern outlines onto a 4x4" sheet of ½" MDO plywood. (We placed a length of transfer paper between the pattern and the plywood, and using a ballpoint pen, traced the pattern onto the plywood. The waxless and greaseless lines of transfer paper don't smudge like most carbon paper. Crafts and art-supply stores usually stock this material in rolls, as do many mail-order firms. You also may use a dressmaker's tracing wheel to mark the lines.)

2. Using an electric hand saber-saw equipped with a plywood-cutting blade, saw out the large body and the two tails. (We supported our plywood on two sawhorses.) Before making the two inside cuts, drill ½" blade start holes inside the areas.

3. From plywood scrap, cut two 2x12" cleats. Using #6x¾" flathead wood screws, attach one cleat to each tail, and then attach them in place on the sides of each cat where indicated.

4. Fill any voids in the edges with wood putty. Next, paint the back and edges with two coats of exterior black paint. When dry, apply two coats of flat white exterior paint to the front surface. (Because of MDO's smooth surface, we roughed up the faces with 120-grit sand-paper before applying our first paint coat.)

5. After these paints have dried, position the patterns on the cutout. Using the same technique described in Step 1, transfer all of the pattern details onto the cutout.

Begin with the ginger cat

Face: Paint White. Add Black whisker dots, muzzle, and eyes. Paint tongue Lisa Pink. Highlight nose with White.

Fur, paws: Orange with Burnt Sienna stripes.

Ears: Burnt Sienna with Lisa Pink inside.

Jacket: Kelly Green.

Pants: Forest Green.

Scarf: Kelly Green, Yellow stripes.

Shoes: Raw Sienna with Burnt Sienna soles.

Song book: White with Kelly Green leaves. Napthol Red Light poinsettia and Yellow berries.

continued

A word about materials, brushes, decorative painting, and patterns

We painted this project on ½" medium-density overlay (MDO) plywood because of its exceptionally smooth surface and its well-deserved reputation among sign painters for withstanding winter's elements. What makes MDO different? A fiberlike paper treated with resin protects both surfaces. Many lumberyards stock MDO in 4x8 sheets and sell it for about $42. You may also find Medex, a vinyl-coated plywood selling for about $32, in some parts of the country. If you choose less expensive exterior plywood, you'll have to spend more time preparing the surface.

For the decorative painting, we chose acrylic paints, available from crafts stores and some hardware and variety stores. Our paint names correspond to Ceramcoat by Delta colors; you may need your retailer's color conversion chart to find names for similar colors sold by other paint manufacturers. To simplify the project, we stuck to basic "color book painting"—no shadows or highlights. For good coverage you may have to apply two or more coats of paint. However, because acrylic paints dry in about 20 minutes, you can move right along. Just keep in mind that the paints will dry quickly in the brush, too. So, wash your brushes frequently.

We used three brushes for this project: a 1"-wide flat brush for large areas such as the jackets, a No. 7 round brush for painting smaller areas and to bring paint right up to the edge, and a No. .3 brush for details such as the holly leaves. So, it wouldn't be unusual for you to use two brushes to paint some of the areas.

A Sanford Sharpie marker or Speedball acrylic Painter marker works great for the black lines that outline the clothing and animals.

HARK, THE HERALD CRITTERS SING!

continued

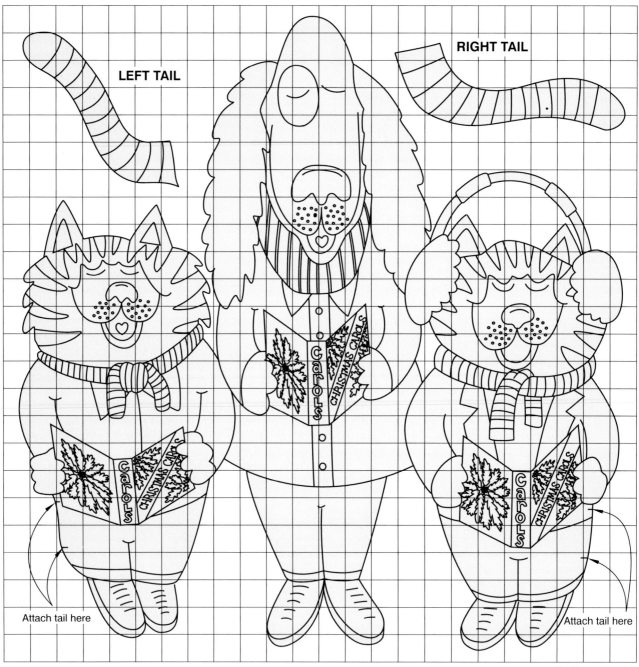

RIGHT TAIL

LEFT TAIL

Attach tail here

Attach tail here

Each square = 2"

It's the dog's turn next

Face: White with Red Iron Oxide spot. Paint whisker dots, muzzle, and eyes Black. Add Lisa Pink tongue and White nose highlight.

Ears, paws: Red Iron Oxide.

Turtleneck: Mix Colonial Blue and White 1:1. Add stripes with technical pen or marker.

Jacket: Laguna with Yellow buttons.

Pants: Mix Colonial Blue and Prussian Blue 1:1.

Shoes, songbook: See ginger cat.

Now, the gray tabby sings

Face: As previously painted.

Fur: Hippo Gray with Black stripes.

Ears: Black with Lisa Pink inside.

Sweater: Lisa Pink.

Jacket: Vintage Wine.

Pants: Liberty Blue and Lisa Pink mixed 1:1.

Scarf, ear muffs: Lilac Dusk with Vintage Wine stripes on scarf. Raw Sienna metal bands with Burnt Sienna adjusters.

Shoes, songbook: See ginger cat.

Just a few finishing touches left

1. Using the photo on *page 4* and your pattern as a guide, apply the black outlines and markings with a Sanford Sharpie marker, a Speedball acrylic Painter marker, or similar black marker. Touch up the black-painted edge of the cutout as necessary.

2. After the paint dries, lightly sand the surface with a Kraft paper sack to remove the fuzz raised by the acrylic paint. Next, apply two protective coats of clear, exterior grade polyurethane. Let the finish dry thoroughly between coats.

3. With glue and screws, attach the 1X3" pine or plywood scrap braces to the back of the ornament as shown *below*. Rip and crosscut two 3X25" braces and hinge them to the cleats. Attach the strap hinges where shown.

4. To anchor the ornament in your yard, fold back the support braces and drive 20-penny nails through the holes in the hinges and into the ground.

Project Tool List

Tablesaw
Portable sabersaw

Note: *We built the project using the tools listed. You may be able to substitute other tools or equipment for listed items you don't have. Additional common hand tools and clamps may be required to complete the project.*

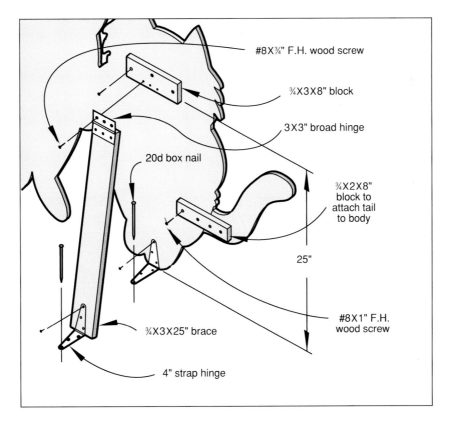

#8X¾" F.H. wood screw

¾X3X8" block

3X3" broad hinge

20d box nail

¾X2X8" block to attach tail to body

25"

¾X3X25" brace

#8X1" F.H. wood screw

4" strap hinge

CARVE A HOLIDAY ANGEL

Celebrate the yuletide season with this festive and versatile pattern from the Heartland's Ron Mackey.

At Ron Mackey's home in Lincoln, Nebraska, every workday has a holiday theme. Ron carves Christmas items in the summer heat, switches to Easter in winter's cold, and fits other holidays in between.

Ron began carving full-time in 1985. Inspired by his wife Leeta's Christmas ornament collection, his career took off. He now sells his work in 14 states and his designs to the likes of Hallmark Cards.

Although many of Ron's pieces reflect a folk-art carving style, his real love lies in classical European carving. "The angel is a perfect example," Ron says. "It's all knife and gouge work. No finishing with sandpaper allowed!" And, true to old-world craftsmanship, he carves *all* surfaces, including backs and edges, "So they feel good."

Choose the size of your angel, then start carving

By enlarging the tree-ornament angel pattern shown about three times, you'll have the makings of a dandy wall plaque or door hanging. Or, reduce it about 40 percent for a lapel-pin-sized carving.

To make an ornament, start with a ⁷⁄₁₆x3¾x5½" piece of basswood. Transfer the pattern to the wood, and cut out the rough with a bandsaw. Next comes the hardest part, according to Ron.

"Drill the hole between the neck, hand, and shoulder with a Forstner bit or a brad-point, the size depending on the angel you're making (pin, ³⁄₃₂"; ornament, ⁵⁄₁₆"; plaque, ½" overlapping holes). Use a gouge or knife to re-shape the round hole," Ron advises.

Next, cut down the surface of the angel's back wing. "The more you lower it, the more shadow effect you'll get," says the carver. Ron shaved this angel's wing by one third the wood thickness—about ¼". Then, redraw the feather lines.

With a knife, make the stop cuts that outline the feathers on both wings. Next, shape them with a flat chisel gouge and a small No. 5 or 7 shallow U-gouge.

Using a No. 5 gouge, carve the depths of the gown drapery with long flowing cuts. "You're actually carving shadows," says Ron.

After you complete the wings and gown, turn to the hair and carve it as you did the wings. To shape the face, start at the chin with a U-gouge and cut a chamfer in one continuous motion up to the forehead. Then, make a gouge for the eye socket. With a knife or V-tool, cut a notch for the eye. "If you chip the trumpet," Ron notes, "give her a smaller horn."

Antiquing a heavenly finish

For a clear finish, Ron applies a cabinetmaker's wax over a light stain or oil. To paint the angel, apply a coat of white acrylic.

Add a wash of light blue and other colors for hair, horn, and face. Then, spray on lacquer. Antique it by lightly sanding or scraping raised portions and edges. Finally, put on a coat of dark, liquid Watco satin finish wax and wipe it off while still wet.

Project Tool List
Bandsaw
Carving knife
Gouges
  ¼" No. 3
  ¼" No. 5
  ⅛" No. 7
V-tool, ⅛"
Portable drill
  Bit size: see text

Note: We made the project using the tools listed. You may be able to substitute other tools or equipment for listed items you don't have. Additional common hand tools and clamps may be required to complete the project.

FULL-SIZED PATTERN
← DIRECTION OF GRAIN →

Other carving block sizes: plaque, 16½ x 12 x 1¼"; pin, 2¼ x 1¾ x ¼"

HEIRLOOM TREE ORNAMENTS

Michael Mode's wife, Kathryn, had a simple request just before Christmas, 1983, "Why not turn a few ornaments to decorate the tree?" Being a dutiful husband, this creative turner went to the shop and emerged a few hours later bearing gifts like the ones shown here. Since then, Mike has turned at least 8,000 ornaments to add to his crafts-fair inventory. Here's how he turns and paints these lovely tree trimmers.

Michael Mode

Tools of the Trade

Mike employs four turning tools to make the ornaments: a 1" gouge to turn the blank round; a ½" gouge to refine the shape; a ⅜" fingernail gouge for the beads, coves, and hollows; and a ½" skew, for the tapers, broad convex shapes, and deep valleys.

Turning the stock to shape

Begin with a piece of yellow poplar 1¾" square by 6" long. Find center on one end, drill a pilot hole there, and mount the stock to a screw center. To avoid hitting the center when turning, leave a small waste block next to the faceplate.

continued

9

HEIRLOOM TREE ORNAMENTS
continued

After making numerous ornaments, Mike has several tips. "First, partially turn the bottom—the portion farthest from the headstock," instructs Mike. "Then, work on the middle and the top. Finally, repeat the process starting at the bottom again. If you turn one area completely, the ornament may get too thin and snap. If you don't have a screw center, turn the ornament between centers with the top (screw-eye end) against the tailstock. The tailstock center mark will eventually become the point of insertion for the screw eye." Use the full-sized patterns to turn your own ornaments.

Sand and paint

Sand the piece with 220-grit paper, and paint the ornament on the lathe, with the lathe running at around 600 rpm. Mike has had the best luck with stiff-bristle brushes, about ¼" long by ¼" wide. "I use water-based acrylic paints of thick consistency, about like cream. Apply the paint heavily, just short of the coloring flying off."

After the paint dries, remove the ornament from the lathe, and cut off the scrap end. Sand and paint the ends. Finally, insert a small screw eye and hang.

Project Tool List

Lathe
    Screw drive center
    1" roughing gouge
    ⅜", ½" spindle gouges
    ½" skew

Note: *We built the project using the tools listed. You may be able to substitute other tools or equipment for listed items you don't have. Additional common hand tools and clamps may be required to complete the project.*

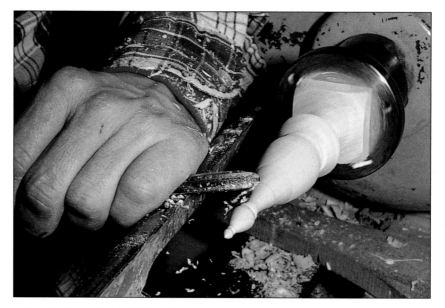

FULL-SIZED HALF PATTERNS

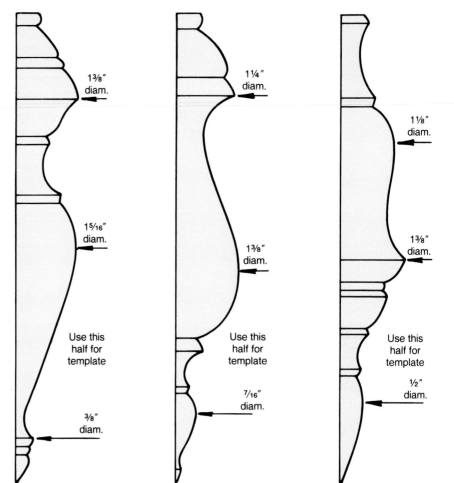

1⅜" diam.

1⁵⁄₁₆" diam.

Use this half for template

⅜" diam.

1¼" diam.

1⅜" diam.

Use this half for template

⁷⁄₁₆" diam.

1⅛" diam.

1⅜" diam.

Use this half for template

½" diam.

SEASONAL SILHOUETTES

S pruce up your Christmas tree this year with these delightfully dainty decorations. You can turn out a treeful in an evening or two with just a little help from your scroll saw and a drill press. While you're at it, cut out a few for your friends and relatives; they'll be glad you did.

Note: You'll need some thin stock for this project. You can resaw or plane thicker stock to size.

Cutting the rings

1. With a compass, mark a 2¾"-diameter circle on ⅛"-thick plywood for each ring required. Reset the compass for a 3"-diameter circle. Now, using the same center point, mark a larger circle outside each smaller one.

2. Chuck a circle cutter into your drill press. Position the cutter where shown on the drawing *above right.* As shown in the photo at *right,* clamp the plywood to the drill table, and position the circle-cutter bit directly over the center-point used to mark the circles. Start the drill (we used a speed of about 250 rpm) and cut halfway through the plywood.

3. Flip the plywood over, center the bit over the hole just drilled, and finish cutting through the plywood to form the inside of the *continued*

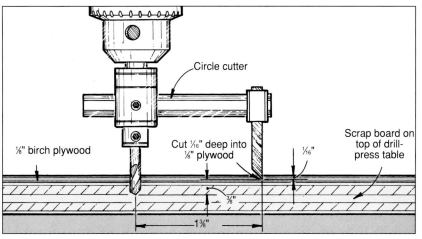

Circle cutter

⅛" birch plywood

Cut ¹⁄₁₆" deep into ⅛" plywood

Scrap board on top of drill-press table

¹⁄₁₆"

⅜"

1⅜"

Use a circle cutter chucked into your drill press to cut the inside of each plywood ring to shape.

SEASONAL SILHOUETTES
continued

ring. The two-step procedure minimizes chip-out.

4. Cut the outside of each ring to shape on a bandsaw or scrollsaw, cutting just outside the marked line. Hand-sand to the line for finished shape (we used a sanding block with 150-grit sandpaper).

5. Cut two pieces of ¾" plywood to 5x7", and construct the drilling jig shown *right*.

6. Clip the head off a 4d finish nail, and chuck the nail into the drill press. Start the drill, and sand or file the bottom ⅜" of the nail to ¹⁄₁₆" diameter. Most ¹⁄₁₆" bits are too small for a drill-press chuck. (We attached 60-grit sandpaper to a sanding block to shape the end of the nail.) Place a ring in the kerf in the jig, center the ring under the bit, and drill a ¹⁄₁₆" thread-access hole through each ring as shown in the photo *below right*.

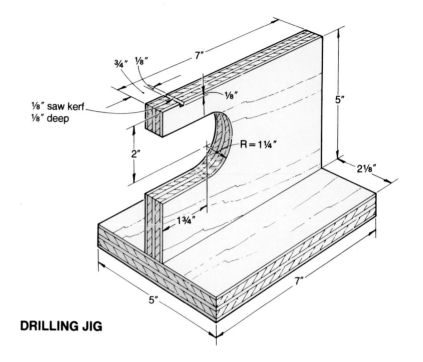

DRILLING JIG

Shaping the holiday figures

1. Using carbon paper, trace the full-sized ornament patterns onto paper. Adhere the patterns to the ⅛" stock with spray adhesive.

2. Scrollsaw the figures to shape, and remove the patterns. If you have trouble removing the paper patterns, moisten them with thinner, and they'll peel right off. Lightly sand each figure with 220-grit sandpaper.

3. With the 4d finish nail still chucked into your drill press, hold a wood figure upright in a handscrew clamp, and drill a ⅛"-deep hole. Later, you'll insert thread into the hole for hanging. See the full-sized patterns for hole locations.

Final assembly

1. Apply the finish of your choice. (For something this small, we prefer an aerosol finish such as a Deft or Flecto product.)

2. Run the thread through the hole in the ring. (We used a heavy-duty, gold-colored cotton thread.) Place a dab of instant glue

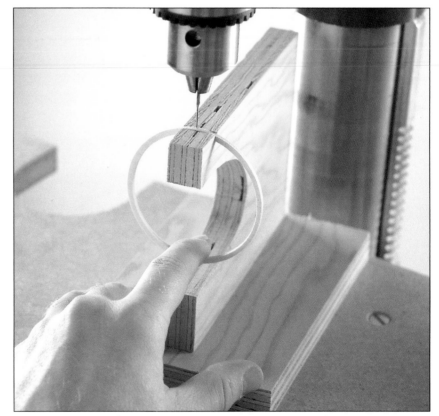

With a sharpened 4d finish nail and a drilling jig, drill a hole through each birch plywood ring.

FULL-SIZED PATTERNS

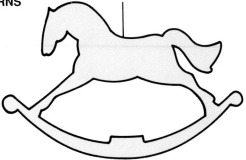

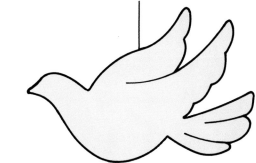

(cyanoacrylate) on the end of the thread inside the ring, and insert the thread into the hole in the top of the hardwood figure. Move the thread up and down to center the figure in the ring. Once properly positioned, put a dab of instant glue on the thread where it goes through the plywood ring.

Project Tool List
Tablesaw
Scrollsaw
Drill press
   Circle cutter

Note: *We built the project using the tools listed. You may be able to substitute other tools or equipment for listed items you don't have. Additional common hand tools and clamps may be required to complete the project.*

TWELVE SCROLLSAWED DAYS OF CHRISTMAS

If you're like most of us, you spend more hours in the shop between now and December 25 than any other time of the year. So we thought you'd enjoy a project you can whip up in an afternoon—four gifts at a time.

1. Rip and crosscut ⅛" or ⁵⁄₃₂" birch plywood into eight strips 4" wide and 18" long. (See the Buying Guide for a source.) Next, make two stacks of four strips, and align the edges and ends. To secure the stacks, drive 4d nails through the pieces.

2. Make copies of the 12 ornament patterns *opposite* and on *page 16*. (We photocopied our patterns.) With spray adhesive, adhere the patterns to the stacks.

3. Drill ¹⁄₁₆" start holes in the backgrounds, and ³⁄₃₂" ribbon holes in the tops. Scrollsaw the pieces to shape. (We used a No. 5 scrollsaw blade for all of our cuts. By stack-cutting the ornaments, we minimized the problem of the blade wandering in thin stock.)

4. Sand to remove fuzz created by the scrollsawing. (We hand-held our palm sander fitted with 120-grit sandpaper.)

5. Finish as desired. (Because the ornaments will be handled only once or twice a year, we left ours unfinished. However, you may prefer the appearance of a painted or sprayed satin finish.) Finally, tie a ¼" ribbon or gold braid through each hole. Hang as desired.

Buying Guide
• Two 2x2' sheets ⁵⁄₃₂" Finnish birch plywood. Enough for 96 ornaments. Stock No. 9703. For current prices, contact Meisel Hardware Specialties, P.O. Box 70, Mound, MN 55364-0700, or call 800-441-9870.

Project Tool List
Scrollsaw
Portable drill
  ¹⁄₁₆" bit
Finishing sander

Note: *We built the project using the tools listed. You may be able to substitute other tools or equipment for listed items you don't have. Additional common hand tools and clamps may be required to complete the project.*

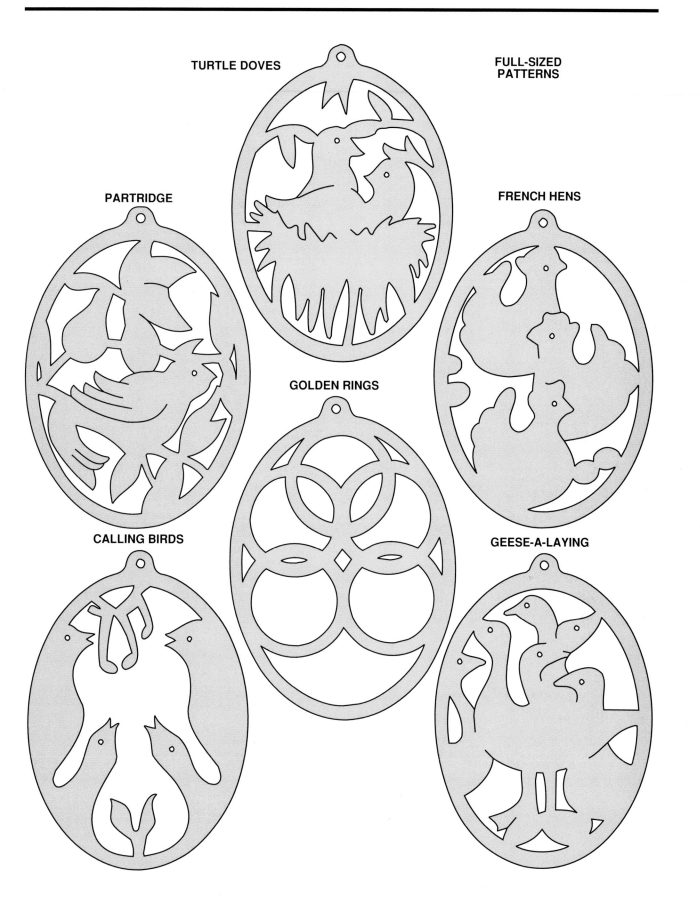

TURTLE DOVES

FULL-SIZED
PATTERNS

PARTRIDGE

FRENCH HENS

GOLDEN RINGS

CALLING BIRDS

GEESE-A-LAYING

continued

TWELVE SCROLLSAWED DAYS OF CHRISTMAS
continued

MAIDS A-MILKING

FULL-SIZED PATTERNS

SWANS A-SWIMMING

DANCERS DANCING

PIPERS PIPING

LORDS A-LEAPING

DRUMMERS DRUMMING

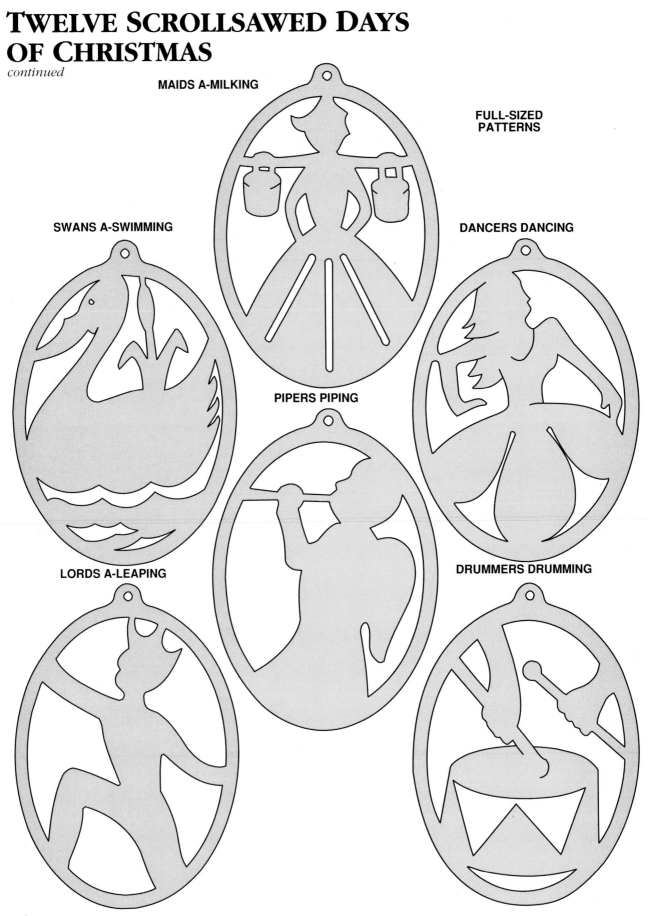

SWEET-TOOTH SANTA

We can't imagine December without sweets, can you? This jolly man will attract all sorts of attention when you keep his belly full of nuts and candies.

continued

SWEET-TOOTH SANTA
continued

Palette

Delta Ceramcoat Colors

BR Burgundy Rose
    Black
BG Black Green
FG Forest Green
IV Ivory
ME Mendocino
MF Medium Flesh
QA Queen Anne's Lace

SB Sweetheart Blush
TR Trail
    White

Brushes

2" foam
No. 4 synthetic flat
No. 12 synthetic flat

Supplies

1x8x13" pine
½x3½x14" pine
¼x4x8" pine
Oil-based Burnt Umber
Odorless turpentine
Crafts knife
Matte-finish varnish
Clothespins

Preparation

After duplicating the patterns on *pages 19* and *21* with tracing paper, copy the Santa outline onto pine (actual size: ¾x7¼"). Cut out Santa with a bandsaw or scrollsaw blade for a smooth cut.

Cut out the following pieces from ½" white pine: two 3⅞x3½" sides, a 5⅛x3½" front, and a 6⅛x4⅛" bottom. (Ask for drawerside material at the lumberyard or plane thicker stock to size.) Dry-assemble the pieces to check the fit. (See the Exploded View drawing on *page 20*.) Then, glue the box with

yellow woodworker's glue, and clamp with rubber bands: Wipe off glue squeeze-out with damp rag, and check that the box dries with 90° joints. Now, transfer the Santa details, trees, and letters to ¼" pine, and cut out the pieces.

With a crafts knife or 50-grit sandpaper, remove the hard edges. Sand all surfaces smooth with 80- and then 150-grit sandpaper. Remove dust with a tack cloth, and seal with a water-based varnish. Then, copy the pattern features with transfer paper.

Painting

Note: Thin all paint with 20 percent water unless otherwise noted. Use a 2" foam brush to base-coat large areas, and the No. 12 flat brush or the No. 4 flat brush for smaller areas.

Santa: Base-coat the face and nose MF. Apply QA to the beard, mustache, cuffs, hat fur, and ball. Paint Santa's coat BR and the gloves BG. Mix White and SB 1:1 and paint Santa's cheeks and mouth.

Use sandpaper to remove enough paint along the edges to allow some wood to show through.

NOEL

With the No. 4 flat brush, paint IV eyebrows. Then, add Black eyes with the handle end of a brush.

Using the No. 12 flat brush, define an arm by floating ME, diluted 1:1 with water, where shown on the pattern. Shade Santa's coat, hat, and beard with a float of ME.

To antique around the beard, coat, and hat, mix oil-based Burnt Umber and odorless turpentine 1:3. Wrap a cotton rag around your index finger, and wipe on a thin coat of the mixture. (Our artist uses her finger to dab an extra touch of Burnt Umber close to the edge of the beard, then pulls it into the coat with the rag.)

Dot the beard with IV. (Our artist uses a plastic four-dot marking tool sold at crafts stores for about $3.)

Box: Base-coat the box with TR. Apply FG trees and ME hearts with a No. 4 flat brush. Add the White dots with the handle end of a brush. Then, antique as described above. With a rag, apply oil-based Burnt Umber to the two tree trunks. Dilute FG with 20 percent water, and wash the color onto the trees and letters. Dot the letters with IV.

Finishing Touches

Glue on the letters, trees, and Santa's features. (For better adhesion, sand the back of each piece with 50-grit sandpaper.) Clamp with clothespins wherever possible, and remove glue squeeze-out with a damp cloth. After the glue dries, apply two coats of a water-based finish.

Project Tool List
Tablesaw
Bandsaw or scrollsaw
Finishing sander

Note: We built the project using the tools listed. You may be able to substitute other tools or equipment for listed items you don't have. Additional common hand tools and clamps may be required to complete the project.

continued

SWEET-TOOTH SANTA
continued

EXPLODED VIEW

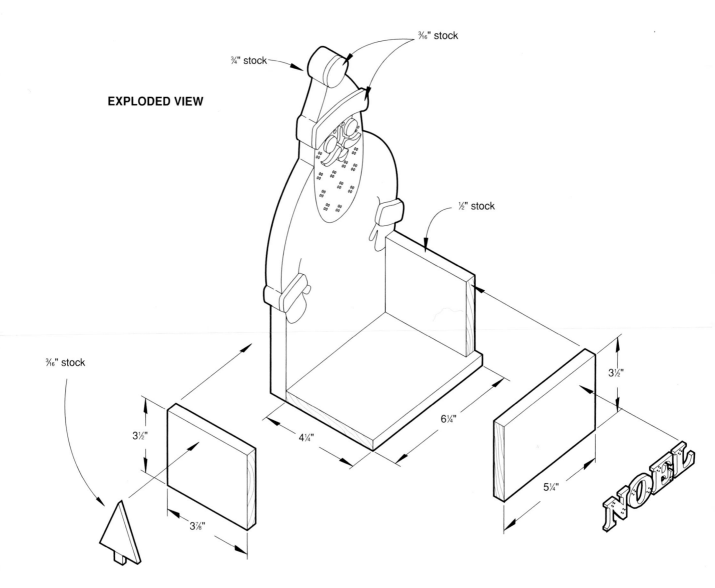

¾" stock

³⁄₁₆" stock

½" stock

³⁄₁₆" stock

3½"

3⅞"

4¼"

6¼"

3½"

5¼"

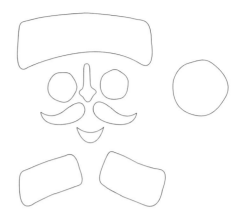

FULL-SIZED PATTERN

DECK THE HALLS

And your table, too, with festive napkin rings when you entertain family and friends during the holidays.

Preparation

Enlarge the patterns *opposite*. Duplicate the patterns with tracing paper. Copy the outlines with transfer paper onto a 6½" square of ³⁄₁₆" Baltic birch plywood.

With a 1"-diameter bit, bore the two napkin holes. Then, cut out the pieces with a scrollsaw, using a No. 5 blade. Or, use a bandsaw with a ⅛" blade.

Sand all surfaces, in the direction of the grain, using 100- and then 150-grit sandpaper. Remove the sanding dust with a tack cloth, and seal all surfaces with wood sealer. Let the sealer dry, sand again, and remove dust with a tack cloth.

Painting

Base-coat large areas with a No. 4 flat brush, and fill in small shapes with a No. 2 flat brush. Apply details with No. 0 and No. 2/0 liner brushes.

Lady: Base-coat her face LP, her coat and bonnet PC, her songbook TW, and her mittens EG. Mix TW and IB 1:1, and paint the fur trim on her coat and bonnet and her bonnet bow. Mix YO and TW 1:1,

and apply her hair. Fill in the eye areas with TW.

With a No. 2 flat brush and RS, shade her hair. Apply TW hair highlights, and paint her eyebrows RS. (Refer to the photograph *above* for guidance.)

Mix IB and PC 1:1, and shade under her bow, under her coat cape, and around her book. Dip the handle end of a brush into YO, and dot her coat buttons.

With a scruffy old brush and an up-and-down pouncing motion, stipple TW on the coat and bonnet fur. Shade her bonnet bow with a 1:1 mixture of TW and IB.

Palette

Liquitex Artist Colors
BS Burnt Sienna 127
EG Emerald Green 450
IB Ivory Black 244
LP Light Portrait Pink 810
PB Phthalocyanine Blue 316
PC Perm. Aliz. Crimson 116
RS Raw Sienna 330
TW Titanium White 432
YO Yellow Oxide 418

Brushes

No. 4 synthetic flat
No. 2 synthetic flat
No. 0 synthetic liner
No. 2/0 synthetic liner

Supplies

³⁄₁₆x6½x6½" Baltic birch
   plywood
Wood sealer
Fine-tipped permanent black
   marking pen
Matte-finish varnish

1" holes

Lightly blush her cheeks with PC, and apply PC lips. Outline her eyes and nose with RS. Paint her pupils PB. Then, dip a stylus or toothpick into TW, and dot eye highlights and a lower-lip highlight.

Gentleman: Base-coat his face LP, his coat PC, his songbook TW, his mittens EG, his hat IB, and his eyes TW. Mix RS and BS 1:1, and fill in his hair, his moustache, and his eyebrows.

Shade his hair and moustache with BS, then apply YO highlight streaks. Mix IB and PC 1:1, and shade under his collar and around his book. Dip the handle end of a brush into YO, and dot his coat buttons. Apply YO collar trim.

Paint his hatband PC, then highlight the top of his hat and the hat brim with TW.

Lightly blush his cheeks with PC. Mix PC and LP 1:1, and apply to his bottom lip. Outline his eyes and

nose tip with RS, and fill in his pupils with BS. With a stylus or toothpick and TW, dot eye highlights.

Books and holly: Mix TW and IB 1:1, and shade along the book spine and page edges. Then, copy the lettering and the holly details onto the cutout with *graphite* paper. (Make your own graphite paper by rubbing pencil lead over the back side of your pattern. Ink beads over many transfer papers.) With a fine-tipped permanent black marking pen, apply the lettering.

Base-coat all holly leaves EG. Then, dip a stylus into PC, and dot all berries.

Finishing Touches

Lightly sand with a brown paper sack to remove fuzz raised by acrylic paints. Remove the dust with a tack cloth. Finally, apply two coats of a water-based matte-finish varnish.

For the lady's skirt, fold a cloth napkin in half, fold the two sides to the center, and then pull the napkin through the hole. Arrange the skirt in pleasing folds. For the man's trousers, fold a cloth napkin in half, roll the two sides to the center, and then pull the rolls through the hole.

Project Tool List

Bandsaw or scrollsaw
Portable drill
   1" bit
Finishing sander

Note: *We built the project using the tools listed. You may be able to substitute other tools or equipment for listed items you don't have. Additional common hand tools and clamps may be required to complete the project.*

"JINGLE BELLS" SLEIGH

**First, machine all
the parts**

1. Rip and crosscut a
length of ¾" material (we
used poplar) to 4½x48"
Then, cut a 12" piece off
of one end of the board.

2. Using your tablesaw
or bandsaw, resaw the
12" piece to ½" thick. Also
resaw the long piece so
that you end up with two
pieces of thin stock—one
¼" thick and the other ³⁄₁₆"
thick. (Be sure to set up
your saw carefully for this
operation, and run scrap
material through first to
make sure the stock is of
uniform thickness.)

3. Sand the cut surfaces
of the boards. Transfer all
full-sized patterns on *pages
26* and *27* to tracing paper.
Using carbon paper, transfer the pattern of the runners (A) to the ¼"-thick
piece, the patterns for
the decking pieces (B, C)
to the ³⁄₁₆" piece, and the
pattern for the steering
mechanism (D) to the
½" piece. (Remember to
mark the centerpoints
for the holes.)

4. With a bandsaw
or scrollsaw, cut all the
parts to rough shape.
Then, sand each part to
finished shape with a
disc sander as shown in
the sketch *opposite, top.*
(We also used a drum
sander to smooth some
of the inside curves. We
stuck both runners and
both outside deck pieces
together with cloth-type
double-faced tape, and then
sanded them in pairs to ensure
identical parts.)

5. Drill holes in the deck pieces
and the steering mechanism.
Next, fit a ½" round-over bit in

Santa would be proud,
and so will you when
you make this fanciful sleigh.
Whether you hang this holiday
decoration on your door to
welcome guests, use it as a
centerpiece for holiday
dinners, or give it as a gift, this
little charmer fills the holiday
bill. And you can make several
of them almost as quickly as
you can just one.

your router (see the Round-Over Detail drawing that accompanies the Exploded View drawing on *page 27* for positioning particulars). Rout a partial round-over along the top edge of the steering mechanism.

6. To make the two deck supports (E), rip two ½"-wide strips from a piece of ¾" scrap. Then, crosscut each of the strips to their finished length—6¼".

Now, assemble and finish the sled

1. Clamp both runners in your woodworker's vise, and lay out the location of the deck supports where shown on the Exploded View drawing on *page 27*.

2. Fasten one of the deck supports in your vise, and using the layout marks you just made, glue and nail one of the runners to the deck support as shown in the sketch *below right*. (Drill pilot holes in the runners first; we had trouble with the runners splitting when we didn't do this.) Fasten the other runners to the deck supports.

3. Position the decking pieces atop the supports. Align the holes in the decking over the center of the front support, and center the pieces between the runners. Once you have them arranged correctly, glue and nail the decking to the supports. This project is fragile, so put a support block beneath the supports to help absorb the shock from the hammer blows (see sketch at *far right*).

4. Glue and bolt the steering mechanism to the middle deck board. Then, apply the finish of your choice. And to put the finishing touches on the project, fasten the nylon line to the steering mechanism, secure a bow and some pine cones to the sled, and personalize it with your name or that of one of your friends.

Project Tool List
Tablesaw
Bandsaw or scrollsaw

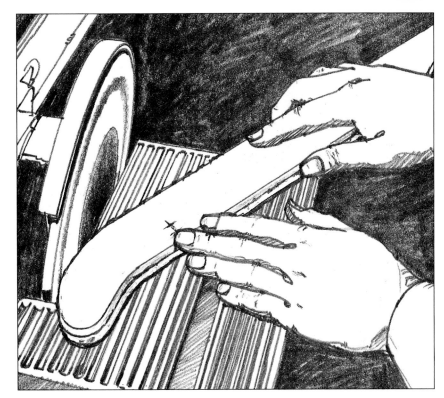

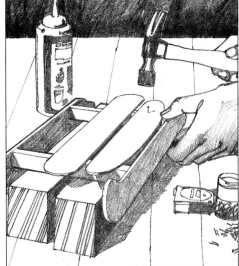

Disc sander
Drill press or portable drill
　Bits: ⅟₁₆", ⅛", ³⁄₁₆"
Router
　Router table
　½" round-over bit
Finishing sander

Note: *We built the project using the tools listed. You may be able to substitute other tools or equipment for listed items you don't have. Additional common hand tools and clamps may be required to complete the project.*

"JINGLE BELLS" SLEIGH
continued

FULL-SIZED PATTERNS

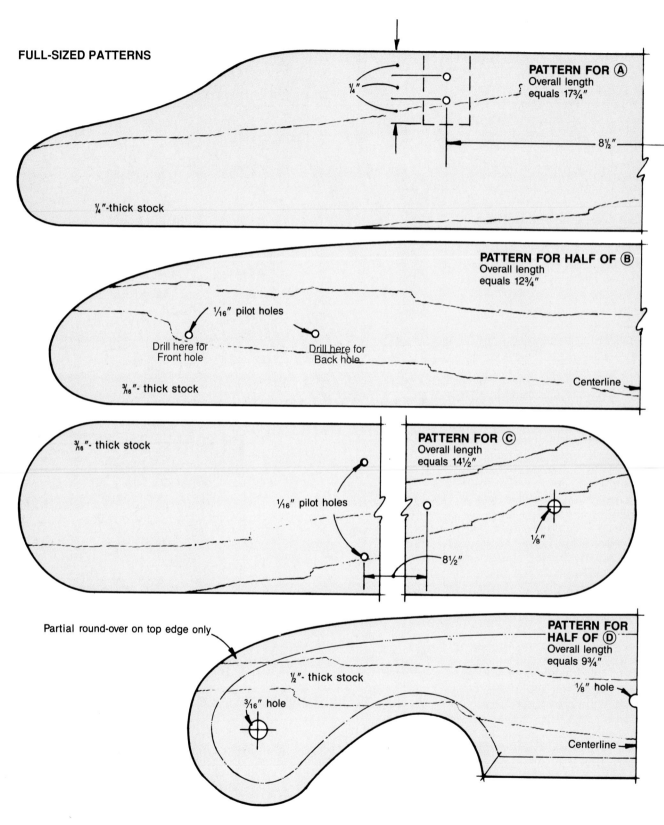

PATTERN FOR Ⓐ
Overall length
equals 17¾"

¼"

8½"

¼"-thick stock

PATTERN FOR HALF OF Ⓑ
Overall length
equals 12¾"

¹⁄₁₆" pilot holes

Drill here for
Front hole

Drill here for
Back hole

Centerline

³⁄₁₆"- thick stock

³⁄₁₆"- thick stock

PATTERN FOR Ⓒ
Overall length
equals 14½"

¹⁄₁₆" pilot holes

8½"

⅛"

Partial round-over on top edge only

**PATTERN FOR
HALF OF Ⓓ**
Overall length
equals 9¾"

⅛" hole

½"- thick stock

³⁄₁₆" hole

Centerline

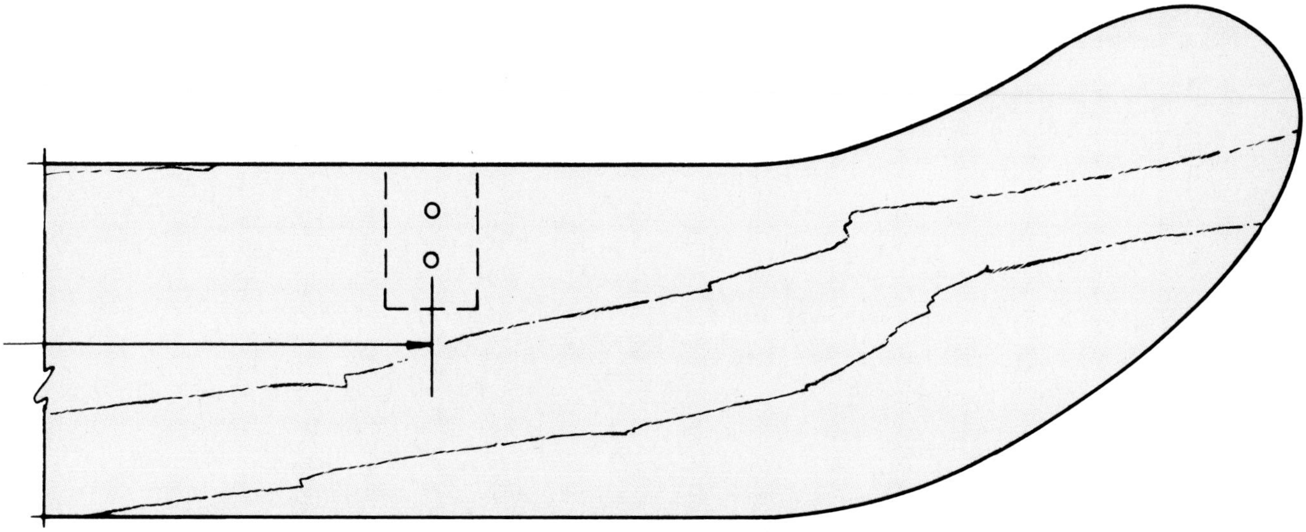

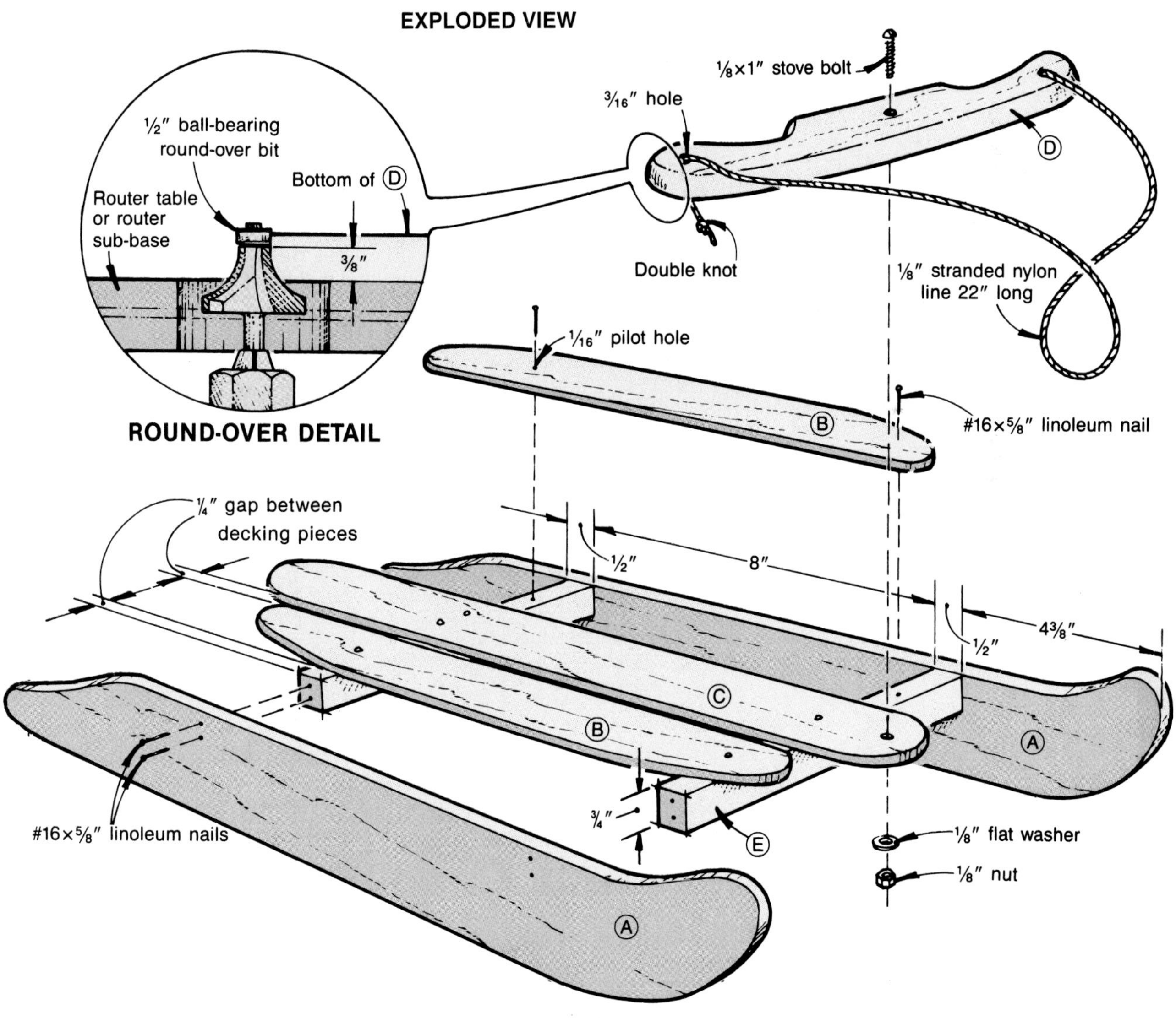
EXPLODED VIEW
1/8×1″ stove bolt
3/16″ hole
D
Double knot
1/8″ stranded nylon line 22″ long
1/2″ ball-bearing round-over bit
Bottom of D
Router table or router sub-base
3/8″
ROUND-OVER DETAIL
1/16″ pilot hole
B
#16×5/8″ linoleum nail
1/4″ gap between decking pieces
1/2″
8″
1/2″
4 3/8″
C
B
A
A
#16×5/8″ linoleum nails
3/4″
E
1/8″ flat washer
1/8″ nut

COLORFUL CHRISTMAS BLOCKS

Center our "Merry Christmas" blocks on the mantel over your fireplace, or some other ideal location, and spread the yuletide spirit. Made from maple, we cut each block 1¾" square, and then finished them in holiday colors.

Note: *To make the 14 blocks shown, we purchased a 2x2x36" turning square. (See the Buying Guide for our source.)*

First, make the blocks

1. Number the sides of your turning square 1, 2, 3, and 4. Next, square your jointer's fence to the table. Using the jointer, surface Side 1 of the square removing ⅛". Place this side snugly against the jointer's fence and surface Side 2 as shown *opposite, left.* Surface Sides 3 and 4 to give the square the 1¾" dimensions shown on the Block drawing *opposite, top right.*

2. Mount a fine-toothed saw blade on your tablesaw and raise it 2" above the tabletop. Clamp a spacer to your fence. (We used scrap ¾" material.) Next, set the fence so the spacer measures 1¾" from the inside of the blade. Adjust your miter gauge for 90° crosscutting, and place the turning square against it. Turn on the saw and square-cut the end of the turning square. Butt the end of the turning square against the spacer, and then push the miter gauge and turning square forward to cut off the first block as shown *below center*. Saw slowly to minimize splintering. Stop the saw and remove the first block. Now, cut thirteen more blocks.

3. Hand-sand the sawed surfaces and edges. Wipe away the dust.

Let's finish the blocks

1. Seal the blocks with a coat of clear finish (we used spray lacquer). This creates a smooth, even surface for the paint. (We sprayed the sides and tops, let them dry, then turned them and sprayed the bottoms.)

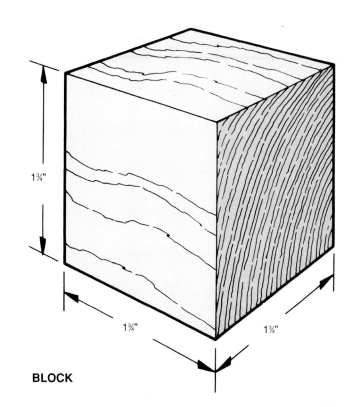

BLOCK

1¾"
1¾"
1¾"

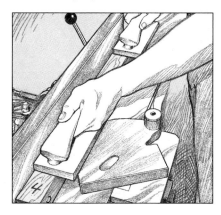

2. Using a 1- to 2"-wide brush, paint the blocks alternating green and red Christmas colors.

3. Once the paint dries, wrap a piece of scrap wood with 220-grit sandpaper and lightly sand the edges of each block with quick, short strokes. (This creates an antique look.) Remove sanding dust.

Note: *We purchased 1¼" tall capital letter stencils (No. 28585) made by Simply Stencils at a local crafts supply store.*

4. Center and firmly hold the stencil for one of the needed letters over a block face and dab on the paint with a stencil brush as shown

above right. (We used antique white for the letters.) Wipe off both sides of the stencil after painting each letter. Move to another block and paint a second letter. Alternate block colors when spelling out the greeting as shown in the photograph *opposite.*

5. Apply two protective coats of a flat matte lacquer or varnish finish. Now, show the blocks off this holiday season and enjoy!

Supplies
Clear finish; acrylic paints in red, green, and white; capital letter stencil; stencil brush.

Buying Guide
• **Hardwood turning square.** One maple 2×2×36", finished two sides. For current prices, contact Constantine's, 2050 Eastchester Road, Bronx, NY 10461, or call 212-792-1600.

Project Tool List
Jointer
Tablesaw

Note: *We built the project using the tools listed. You may be able to substitute other tools or equipment for listed items you don't have. Additional common hand tools and clamps may be required to complete the project.*

HOLIDAY CANDLE HOLDER

Help create a festive holiday spirit with this charming accent. Made from pine, our scrapwood Christmas tree display will brighten any flat surface such as a tabletop or mantel. The set includes the tree-silhouetted candle holder, and three varying-sized trees.

Note: All wood parts for this project can be cut from a ¾X5½X12" piece of pine. See the Cutting Diagram opposite.

First, saw out the parts

1. Place a sheet of carbon paper on a ¾X5½X12" piece of pine. Trace the patterns shown *opposite* for the base (A), the face (B), and the three trees (C, D, E) on the pine.

2. Next, drill the ½" hole ⅜" deep in the base where indicated.

3. Using a scrollsaw or a bandsaw fitted with a ⅛" blade, cut out the five shapes. (To cut out the large tree, we first drilled a ⅛" hole through the workpiece at the tree's tip, inserted the blade through the hole, and then attached the blade to the upper blade clamp.) Next, sand the cut edges smooth to remove the saw marks.

Assemble the candle holder and finish it

1. Attach the face (B) to the base (A). (We clamped the front edge of the base ¾" in from the edge of our workbench. Next, we placed the vertical face piece against it, drilled the pilot holes as shown *above right,* applied glue [we used yellow

woodworker's glue] to the mating surfaces, and then nailed the two pieces together with a pair of No. 16X1" brads.) Set the brads, and plug the holes with wood putty.

2. Apply the finish of your choice to the candle holder and trees. (We used a white, translucent "pickled" finish. To do this, we first diluted a water-based white latex paint and brushed it on the surface.

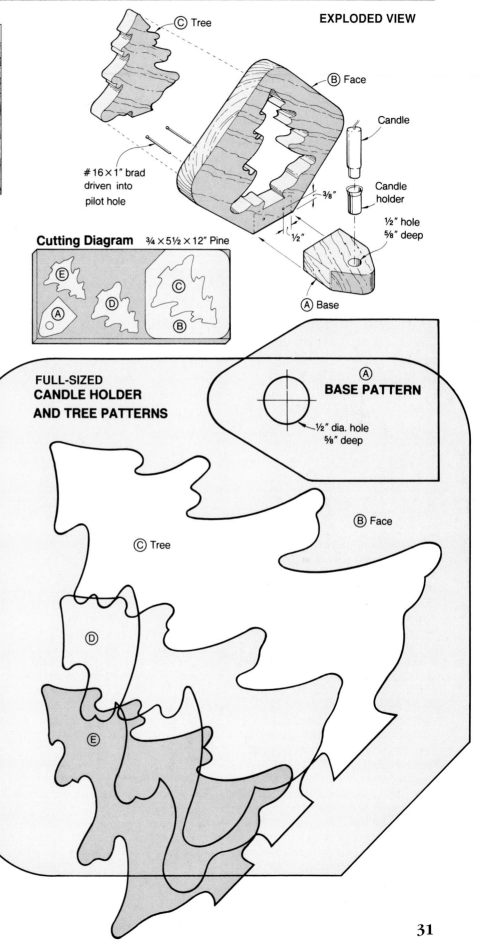

Then, with the paint still wet, we wiped some of it off with a rag, letting some wood grain show through. Once dry, we sprayed on a coat of polyurethane.)

3. Using a pipe cutter, cut off a 1" length of ½" outside-diameter flexible copper pipe. Ream the ends to smooth them with the reamer attachment on the pipe cutter. Next, clamp the piece of pipe in a flaring tool and flare one end as shown *above*. Remove the pipe and friction-fit it in the hole in the base. Insert a candle. (We purchased a ½"-diameter candle from a crafts store and trimmed it with a knife to fit.)

Supplies
White latex paint, pipe cutter, flaring tool for ½" pipe, ½" candle.

Project Tool List
Scrollsaw
Portable drill
    Bits: ¹⁄₁₆", ⅛", ½"
Finishing sander

Note: *We built the project using the tools listed. You may be able to substitute other tools or equipment for listed items you don't have. Additional common hand tools and clamps may be required to complete the project.*

EXPLODED VIEW

Ⓒ Tree

Ⓑ Face

Candle

Candle holder

½" hole
⅝" deep

#16×1" brad driven into pilot hole

⅜"

½"

Ⓐ Base

Cutting Diagram   ¾ × 5½ × 12" Pine

Ⓔ Ⓐ Ⓓ Ⓒ Ⓑ

FULL-SIZED CANDLE HOLDER AND TREE PATTERNS

Ⓐ
BASE PATTERN

½" dia. hole
⅝" deep

Ⓑ Face

Ⓒ Tree

Ⓓ

Ⓔ

CARVED NOEL

Artist and carver Fern Weber prepared this delightful holiday decoration for your woodworking pleasure. It combines scrollsawing and light-duty carving, making it an excellent one-evening project.

First, cut out the parts

1. Rip and crosscut a board to measure ¾×4×12". (We selected butternut for its ease of carving.)

2. Photocopy the NOEL and Holly patterns *opposite*. Cut out the patterns with scissors, and adhere them to the board you cut in Step 1 with spray adhesive. (You can also trace the patterns directly onto the board using carbon paper.)

3. Drill ¼" blade-start holes in the O and the E of NOEL.

4. Clamp a fine-toothed blade to your scrollsaw (we used a No. 5 scrollsaw blade). Saw between the NOEL and the holly parts to separate them.

5. Clamp a temporary fence to your scrollsaw or bandsaw table, and resaw the holly parts to ⅜" thick. Sand the sawn surfaces.

6. Scrollsaw the NOEL to shape. Next, stop the saw and thread the blade through one of the start holes. Cut out this interior area, and then the other. Make all cuts as smooth as possible to reduce the amount of sanding you'll need to do later. Now, scrollsaw the holly parts.

7. Remove the patterns from the parts. (We used lacquer thinner.)

Now, let's carve

Note: *We used a No. 5 (⅜") gouge and a bench carving knife to carve our NOEL and decorative holly.*

1. Using a bench carving knife, cut a 45° bevel along the front outside and inside edges of each letter as shown *below*. Cut with and across the grain, but do not cut into woodgrain. When possible, control your blade with the hand holding the knife, and push against the back of the blade with the thumb of your opposite hand. If the blade slips into wood grain and looks like it may split the wood, back out of the cut and work in the opposite direction. (We used a lap board to hold the workpiece firmly and safely.)

2. Following the dashed line on the NOEL pattern, pencil a line to separate the N and O, the O and E, and the E and L where they touch. Using the point of your knife, cut ⅛" deep into these lines, and then bevel-cut toward them from both sides. Carvers call this backcutting.

3. Sand the face and cut edges of the NOEL, starting with 220-grit sandpaper and moving to 400-grit.

4. Turn to the holly parts and cut ⅛"-deep lines around the penciled berries on the top surface to start the stop cuts. (We used our bench carving knife for these cuts.)

5. Scoop out the scallops on the holly leaves working from point to point, and from the centerlines toward the edges. (We alternated tools, using the bench carving knife and a No. 5 [⅜"] gouge. To reduce slipping while carving, we held the workpieces on a rubberized friction mat.) Backcut to the berries. Next, scallop the back to add shape, but maintain a small, flat area for gluing.

Finish your creation

1. Finish the NOEL. (We brushed on a coat of wood sealer and let it dry 24 hours. Next, we brushed on four coats of poly-urethane, rubbing between coats with 0000 steel wool. Finally, we buffed the letters with very fine steel wool and rubbed in Butcher's paste wax.)

2. Rough-sand the holly leaves with 100-grit sandpaper to remove any unwanted unevenness.

3. Brush a dark green wash paint (we used acrylic-type crafts paint) over the holly leaves and let dry. Add a few strokes of light green over the dark green on each side of the leaf ridges on the top surface. Next, stroke fine branches of dark green along the ridges. Paint the berries cranberry-red.

4. Mark and lightly sand the contact areas on the backs of the leaves and the NOEL. Glue the leaves on with epoxy. If you wish to hang the NOEL, add a picture hanger to the back. Or, let it stand alone in a place of high visibility where loved ones and friends can enjoy it.

Supplies

Epoxy, acrylic paints, finish.

Project Tool List

Tablesaw
Scrollsaw
Bandsaw
Portable drill
  ¼" bit
⅜" No. 5 gouge
Carving knife
Finishing sander

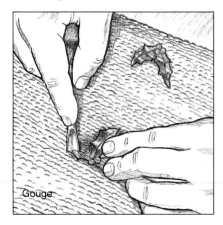

Gouge

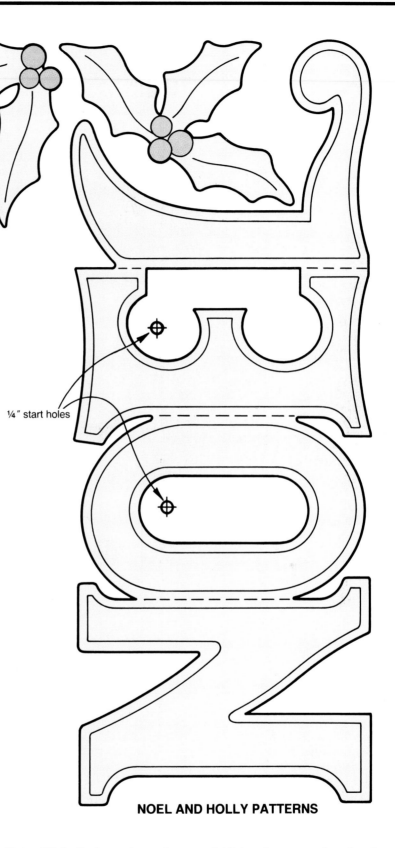

¼" start holes

NOEL AND HOLLY PATTERNS

Note: *We built the project using the tools listed. You may be able to substitute other tools or equipment for listed items you don't have.*

Additional common hand tools and clamps may be required to complete the project.

CHIP-CARVED SNOWMAN

When the weather turns for the worse, why not turn for the better by shaping this handsome, decorative snowman in the cozy confines of your shop. Then to complete, chip-carve the bulbous body and head, and paint. Using our turning template will help ensure your immediate success.

Note: To make our snowman, we started with a 2½x2½x6" basswood turning square and a ⅜x2x2" piece of scrap basswood.

First, turn the snowman to shape

1. Mark the centers on the ends of a 2½x2½x6" basswood turning square. (We drew diagonal lines from the corners with a straight-edge and pencil.) Next, mount the square between centers on your

lathe and turn it to a 2½"-diameter cylinder using a ½" gouge. (We ran our lathe at 800 rpm for this.)

Note: If you wish, exaggerate the snowman's proportions to your own liking. You can also turn a larger snowman by using a larger square.

2. Next, trace a copy of the Snowman Template on *page 36,* including the segment dividing lines, along one edge on a piece of posterboard. (We used carbon paper.) Hold this up to the cylinder, turn on the lathe, and transfer all of the lines to the turning with a pencil as shown at *right*. Cut out the shaded area of the template with scissors.

3. Return to the lathe with a parting tool and cut into the turning to the prescribed depths at the lines you just marked. (We ran our lathe at 1,250 rpm for this.) When parting the body segments, stop ⅛" from the final prescribed depths. Adjust your calipers to the measurements shown on the Snowman Front View on *page 37,* and check each cut. Add ⅛" to the parting dimensions for the three body segments. (We'll cut V-grooves later at these locations after removing more of the excess material.)

4. Beginning at the top or hat, start shaping the hat, narrowing the taper toward the brim. Cut a shallow V-groove ⅛" up from the brim to mark the hatband location. Next, move below the brim and shape the rounded head. Check the diameter. Work the point of the skew into the neck/body joint and form a rounded V-groove to the correct diameter (1¼"). Gently rotate the skew's handle to make the rounding cut. (See drawing *right.)* Go back and shave the hat brim to 2" diameter. Frequently check the work area with an outside calipers until you achieve the correct depth.

5. Move down and turn the middle body segment. Next, cut the rounded V-groove between the middle and lower segment. Finally, cut the rounded V-groove between the lower segment and base. Now, hold the template against the turning to check its shape. Make any corrections needed.

6. Sand the snowman while it spins on the lathe as shown *right.* (We ran our lathe at 1,500 rpm and sanded first with 150-grit sandpaper, then graduating to 220- and 320-grit sandpaper.) With your parting tool, turn the waste areas at each end to ¼". To ensure the snowman will sit flat without rocking, turn a slightly concave bottom up to the ¼" tenon. Remove the turning from the lathe, and cut
continued

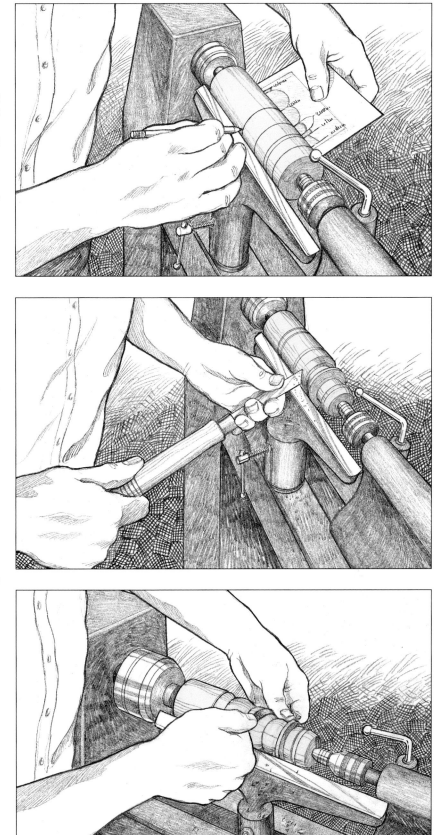

CHIP-CARVED SNOWMAN

continued

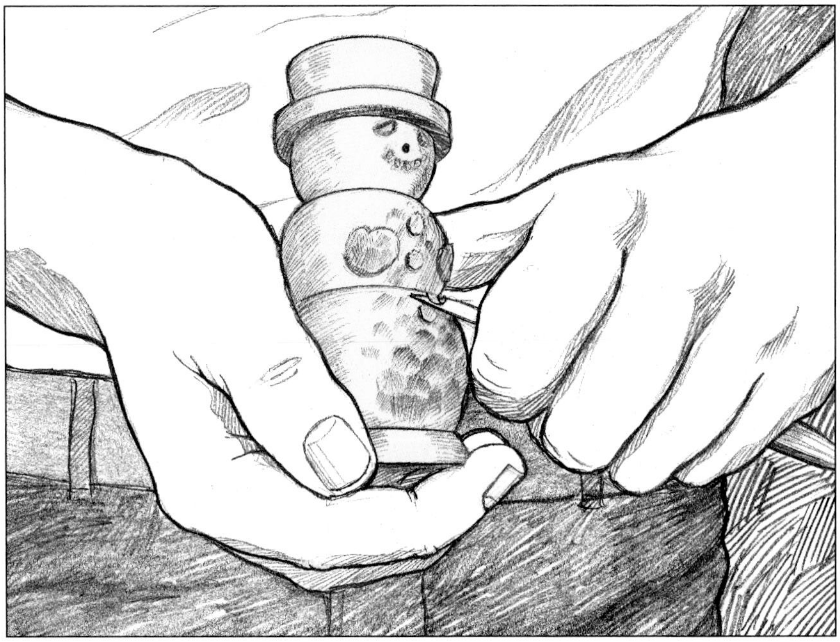

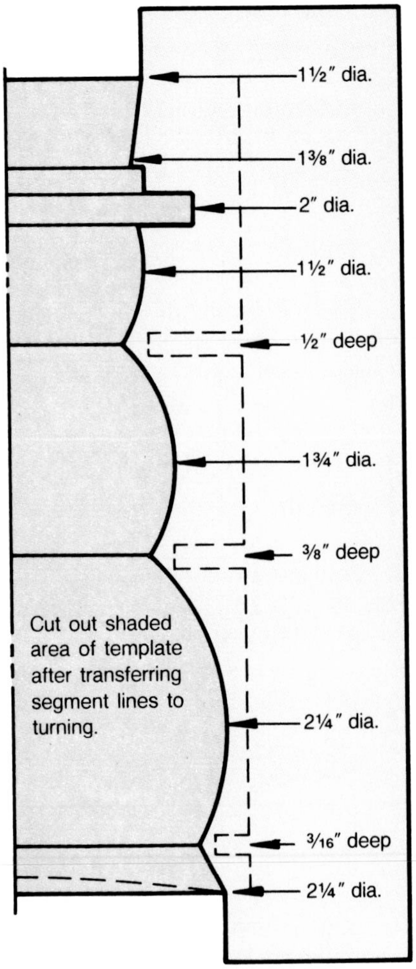
1½" dia.
1⅜" dia.
2" dia.
1½" dia.
½" deep
1¾" dia.
⅜" deep
Cut out shaded area of template after transferring segment lines to turning.
2¼" dia.
3/16" deep
2¼" dia.

SNOWMAN TEMPLATE

off the top waste. Use a ⅜" chisel to cut off the remaining tenon in the concave bottom. Now, sand both of the ends smooth.

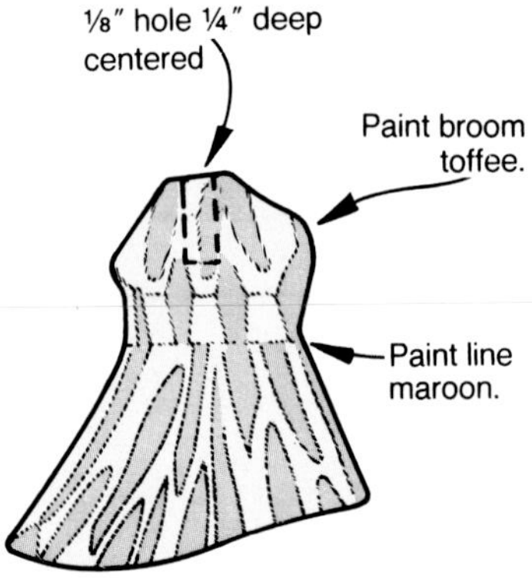
⅛" hole ¼" deep centered
Paint broom toffee.
Paint line maroon.

BROOM PATTERN

Now, carve your snowman

1. Using a pencil and the Snowman Front View drawing *opposite* for reference, mark the locations of the eyes, teeth, buttons, mittens, and hole for the broom handle. Locate the center-point between the eyes and teeth and make a mark for the carrot nose. Using a ⅛" drill bit, bore a hole at this location ¼" deep. Carve the end of a ⅛" dowel to resemble a carrot, and cut this end off at ⅝". (We used a bench carving knife.) Test-fit the nose piece in the hole, and then set it aside until later.

2. Cut around the outlines of the mittens, coal buttons, teeth, and eyes to form stop cuts. (We used a fine V-groove tool and bench carving knife.) The stop cuts let you remove the wood surrounding these parts when chip-carving in order to create relief.

3. Next, with a bench carving knife or flat gouge, chip-carve around the outlined parts and create a faceted surface on the body and head segments. See the drawing *above top*. Do not carve the hat. (We made our carved facets ¼" to ⅜" long.)

4. Carve very small (1/16 to ⅛") facets on the surfaces of the mittens, coal buttons, teeth, and eyes.

5. Poke a starter hole with an awl between the thumb and fingers of the right mitten. (See the Snowman Front View). Now, chuck a 9/64" bit into a portable electric drill, and drill a ¾"-deep hole at a 30° angle to the body.

6. Copy the Broom Pattern, shown *above left*, onto paper and then trace or adhere it to one side of the ⅜"-thick scrap piece of basswood. Drill a ⅛" hole ¼" deep in the edge where indicated on the pattern. Next, cut out the broom piece on a scrollsaw or bandsaw, and chip-carve around it, especially the edges, to give it a more natural shape. Now, start carving the straw texture into your broom's surface with a V-groove tool. (To create the irregular pattern of the broom straw, we cut several grooves measuring ¼" to ¾" long and at slightly different angles.)

SNOWMAN FRONT VIEW
(FULL-SIZED)

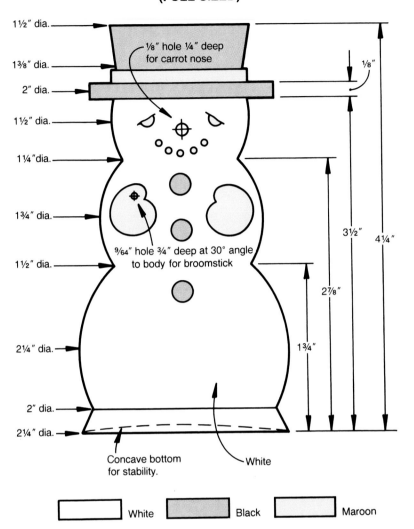

1½" dia.

⅛" hole ¼" deep
for carrot nose

1⅜" dia.

2" dia.

⅛"

1½" dia.

1¼" dia.

3½"

4¼"

1¾" dia.

⁹⁄₆₄" hole ¾" deep at 30° angle
to body for broomstick

1½" dia.

2⅞"

2¼" dia.

1¾"

2" dia.

2¼" dia.

Concave bottom
for stability.

White

| White | | Black | | Maroon |

polyurethane finish. (After that dried we also wiped on a coat of Watco's Satin Dark liquid wax and wiped it off immediately in order to create highlights and a washed look.) After the wax dries, apply a second coat of clear finish to the snowman.

5. For Frosty's scarf, cut a 12" to 14" length of ⅞"-wide cloth or ribbon (we used a colorful red and green plaid) and tie it around the neck. Trim the ends to desired length. Now, look around for a shelf on which to proudly display your newly created holiday decoration.

Note: If you would like to make the snowman into a hanging ornament, turn a small screweye into the center of the hat. Other options include replacing the stove-pipe hat with a stocking cap, enlarging the project or making a variety of sizes, and using small twigs for arms.

Supplies
⅛" dowel, acrylic paints, finish, ⅞x12" piece of cloth.

Project Tool List
Scrollsaw or bandsaw
Lathe
  Spur drive center
  Tail center
  ½" spindle gouge
  ¾" skew chisel
  Parting tool
Portable drill
  Bits: ⅛", ⁹⁄₆₄"
Carving knife
⅛" V-tool

Note: We built the project using the tools listed. You may be able to substitute other tools or equipment for listed items you don't have. Additional common hand tools and clamps may be required to complete the project.

7. From ⅛" dowel, crosscut a 2½" long broom handle. Glue one end of the dowel in the broom. Test-fit the broom handle's point into the hole in the snowman's mitten. Lightly finish-sand all pieces without disturbing the faceted look.

Note: We did not glue the broom handle into the snowman. This way it will be easier to replace should it accidentally be broken or lost.

Liven up your snowman with colorful paint

1. First, brush a base coat of ivory-colored paint over the entire snowman. (We used acrylic paints made by Ceramcoat and available at most well-stocked crafts supply stores.) Paint the hat black. While these coats dry, you can paint the

nose red-orange, the broom toffee (dark tan), and the broom-stick maroon-red, or choose your own colors.

2. Once the broom dries, paint a fine maroon-red line across its midsection to represent the binding holding the straw together. When the paint on the snowman dries, paint the hatband and mittens maroon-red. Paint the coal eyes, teeth, and buttons black. Let dry. To intensify the colors, you may wish to apply two coats of these paints.

3. After the paints dry, glue the carrot in the nose. Insert the broom handle in the hole drilled for it.

4. Now, stand your snowman on a sheet of paper and apply a coat of acrylic or semi-gloss clear

CHRISTMAS TREE ORNAMENTS

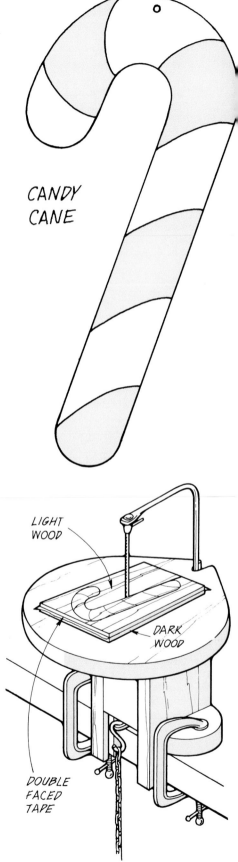

CANDY CANE

Add an extra special touch to your Christmas tree (or someone else's) this year with these fun-to-make wooden ornaments. Trace any or all of our six full-sized patterns or design your own. Either way, these delightful tree trimmers are sure to please.

Note: You'll need some ⅛" stock to make these ornaments. You can resaw or plane thicker stock to size. You can cut and assemble the pieces as explained below, or to simplify the procedure, transfer the full-sized patterns to ⅛" stock. Then, cut the ornaments to shape and paint them.

1. Cut a slightly oversized piece of each type of wood you want to use. Stack the material (the lightest-color species on top), using double-faced tape to adhere the pieces together.

2. Transfer the design to tracing paper, then use carbon paper to transfer it to the stock.

3. Cut through the stacked material with a thin-bladed coping saw or jigsaw.

4. Remove the tape from between the pieces, then assemble the ornaments using the contrasting colors of wood. Glue the pieces together with epoxy. Remove excess glue after it forms a skin and allow to dry.

5. Hand-sand the assembled ornaments with medium- and fine-grit sandpaper, then apply two coats of lacquer or poly-urethane. After the finish dries, drill a ¹⁄₁₆" hole in each ornament; insert string and hang.

Project Tool List
Scrollsaw
Portable drill
  ¹⁄₁₆" bit
Finishing sander

Note: We built the project using the tools listed. You may be able to substitute other tools or equipment for listed items you don't have. Additional common hand tools and clamps may be required to complete the project.

LIGHT WOOD

DARK WOOD

DOUBLE FACED TAPE

TRUMPETING
ANGEL

REINDEER

FULL-SIZED
PATTERNS

WISEMAN

COURT
JESTER

WOODEN
SOLDIER

39

AWAY IN A MANGER

Brighten up your family traditions with our folk-art Nativity set that beams with color.

Preparation

Enlarge the patterns on *pages 42 to 53*, then duplicate the designs with tracing paper. Using transfer paper, copy the manger arch onto 1×12" pine; Mary, Joseph, the camel, and the donkey onto 1×8" pine; the angel, the arch star, and the three

Palette

DecoArt Americana Colors

AG Antique Gold-DA9
AV Avocado-DA52
BG Bluegrass Green- DA47
BR Berry Red-DA19
BU Burnt Umber-DA64
CD Cadmium Red-DA15
CL Coral Rose-DA103
CN Cool Neutral-DA89
CR Country Red-DA18
DC Dark Chocolate-DA65
DG Dove Gray-DA69
DP Diox. Purple-DA101
DR Dusty Rose-DA25
DT Desert Turquoise-DA44
EB Ebony Black-DA67
FG Forest Green-DA50
FT Flesh Tone-DA78
GB Gooseberry Pink-DA27
GC Georgia Clay-DA17
GS Gray Sky-DA111
HG Holly Green-DA48
LA Light Avocado-DA106
LC Light Cinnamon-DA114
LV Lavender-DA34
MF Medium Flesh-DA102
MJ Mint Julep-DA45
MO Mocha-DA60
MT Mink Tan-DA92
MY Moon Yellow-DA7
PU Pumpkin-DA13
RR Rookwood Red-DA97
RS Raw Sienna-DA93
SP Sapphire-DA99
SW Snow White-DA01
TA Tangerine-DA12
TG Teal Green-DA107
UL Ultra Blue Deep-DA100
VB Victorian Blue-DA39
WB Wmsburg.Blue-DA40
YO Yellow Ochre- DA8

Brushes

#12 synthetic flat
#8 synthetic flat
#2 synthetic flat
#0 synthetic liner

Supplies

2x4x7" pine
1x12x16" pine
1x8x26" pine
1x6x42" pine
1x4x40" pine
⅜x28" dowel
Nonwaxed transfer paper
Woodburning tool
Matte-finish spray varnish

wisemen onto 1x6" pine; and baby Jesus, the shepherd, and the three sheep onto 1x4" pine. Cut out the pieces with a scrollsaw, using a No. 9 blade, or use a bandsaw with a ⅛" blade.

Cut ⅜"-diameter dowel as follows: one piece 7" long to attach the star to the arch, one piece 15½" long (this connects the angel to her base), and two pieces each 2" long to attach the arch to its base.

From 2" pine (actual size: 1½" thick), cut a 3x7" base for the angel. To find the center, draw diagonal lines from corner to corner. (The two lines cross at the center.) Now, drill a ⅜" hole 1" deep into the base. From 1x4" pine cut a 15½"-long base for the arch. Drill ⅜" holes in the angel, star, and arch where shown on the patterns. Then, glue the dowels in the arch. Do not glue the arch to its base.

Sand all pieces—including the dowels—with the grain, using 100- and then 150-grit sandpaper. Remove the dust with a tack cloth. Copy the details onto the front and back of each cutout with a nonwaxed transfer paper.

Woodburning the details

Designer Sarah Grant-Hutchison uses a universal tip for burning detail. She suggests that you preheat your woodburning tool and practice on scrap pine before you begin working on the project pieces. To avoid uneven lines, Sarah keeps the tool moving at a consistent pace. Burn in all design lines on both the front and back of each cutout. Join the corresponding lines on each cutout edge to complete the design.

Painting

Choose the brush that best fits into the design area. For example, our artist uses a No. 0 liner brush for mouths and eyes; a No. 2 flat brush for narrow bands on the clothing, for the donkey's reins, and for the shepherd's cane, a No. 8 flat brush for faces, cheeks, hair, and beards; and a No. 12 flat brush for filling in all larger areas of color on the clothing, manger, etc. To make dots on the arch, on Mary's cuffs, and on Joseph's headband, use the handle end of a liner brush.

Thin all paints with water 5:1. Then, follow the palette code shown on each pattern for a guideline. Four pieces are not shown on the patterns: Paint the angel's base CD; mix DP and RR 1:1 and paint the dowel. Paint the dowel connecting the star and arch TG, and apply UL and SW mixed 1:1 to the base.

Finishing touches

Sand all pieces lightly with a paper grocery sack to remove fuzz raised by acrylic paints. With dowels, attach the star to the arch and the angel to its base. (For convenient storage, don't glue these dowels in place.) Finish with two coats of a matte-finish spray varnish.

Project Tool List

Scrollsaw
Portable drill
⅜" bit
Woodburning tool
Finishing sander

Note: *We built the project using the tools listed. You may be able to substitute other tools or equipment for listed items you don't have. Additional common hand tools and clamps may be required to complete the project.*

continued

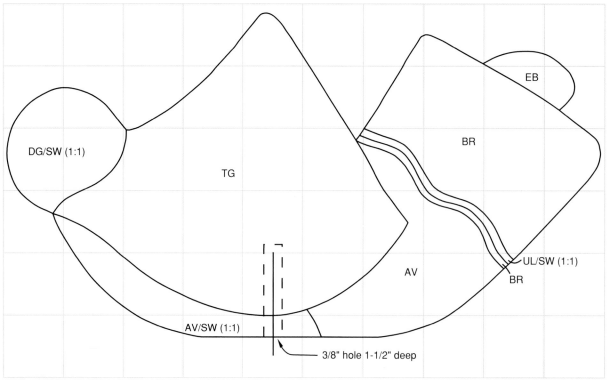

ANGEL BACK   **1 Square = 1 Inch**

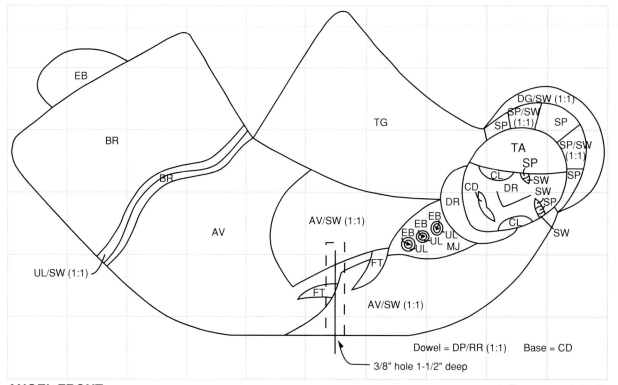

ANGEL FRONT   **1 Square = 1 Inch**

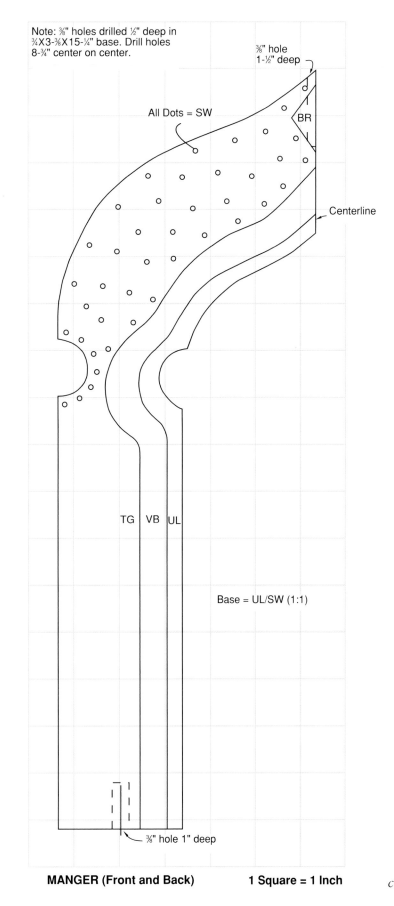

Note: ⅜" holes drilled ½" deep in
¾X3-⅜X15-¼" base. Drill holes
8-¾" center on center.

⅜" hole
1-½" deep

All Dots = SW

BR

Centerline

TG VB UL

Base = UL/SW (1:1)

⅜" hole 1" deep

MANGER (Front and Back)   **1 Square = 1 Inch**   *continued*

AWAY IN A MANGER
continued

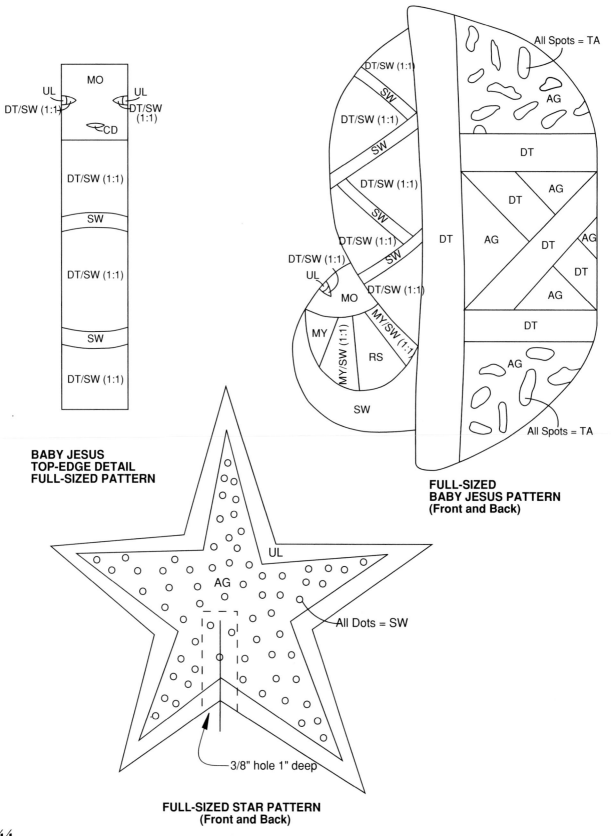

**BABY JESUS
TOP-EDGE DETAIL
FULL-SIZED PATTERN**

**FULL-SIZED
BABY JESUS PATTERN
(Front and Back)**

**FULL-SIZED STAR PATTERN
(Front and Back)**

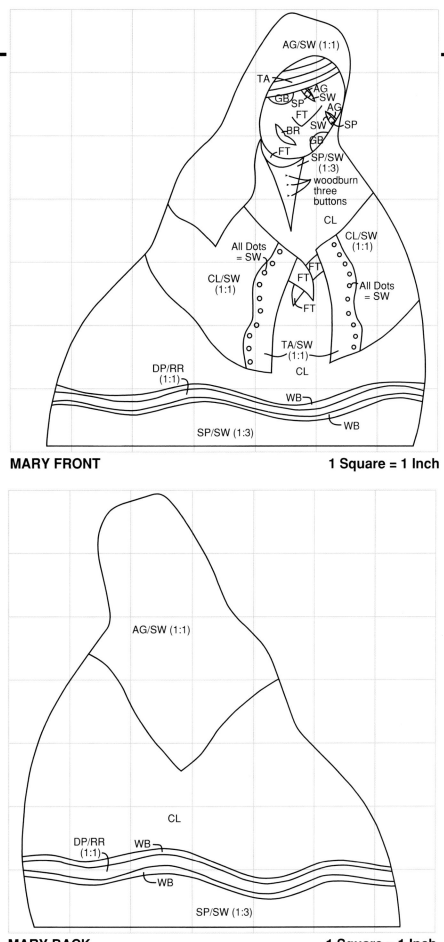

MARY FRONT 1 Square = 1 Inch

MARY BACK 1 Square = 1 Inch

continued

AWAY IN A MANGER
continued

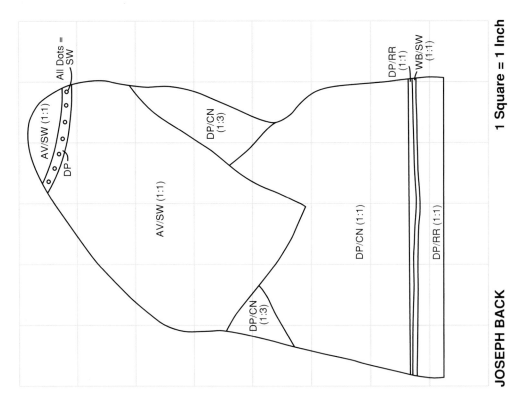

JOSEPH BACK

1 Square = 1 Inch

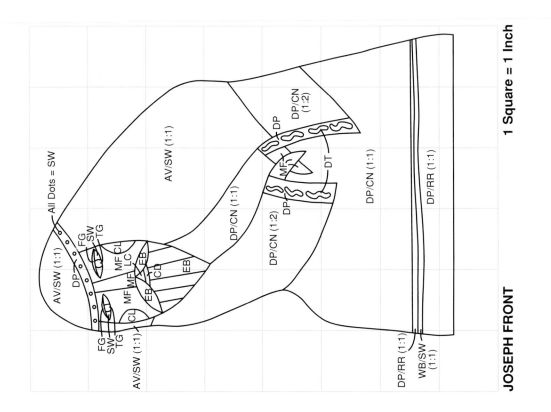

JOSEPH FRONT

1 Square = 1 Inch

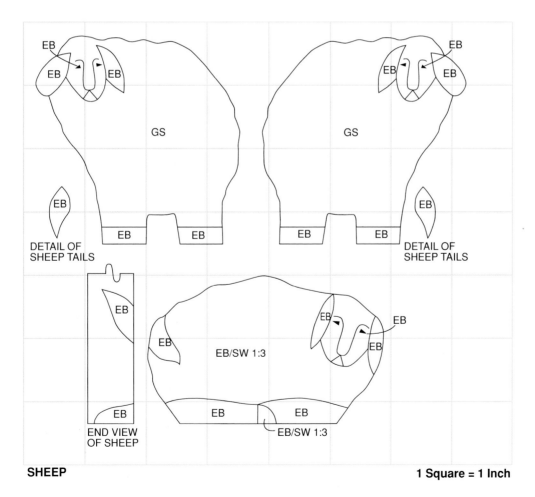

EB

EB   EB

GS

EB

DETAIL OF
SHEEP TAILS

EB   EB

END VIEW
OF SHEEP

EB

EB

EB   EB

EB   EB

GS

EB

EB   EB

DETAIL OF
SHEEP TAILS

EB

EB

EB/SW 1:3

EB   EB

EB/SW 1:3

SHEEP

1 Square = 1 Inch

continued

AWAY IN A MANGER
continued

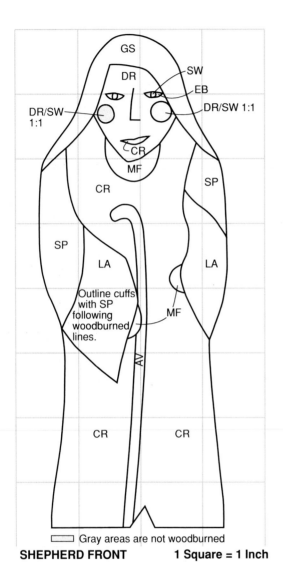

Gray areas are not woodburned

SHEPHERD FRONT   **1 Square = 1 Inch**

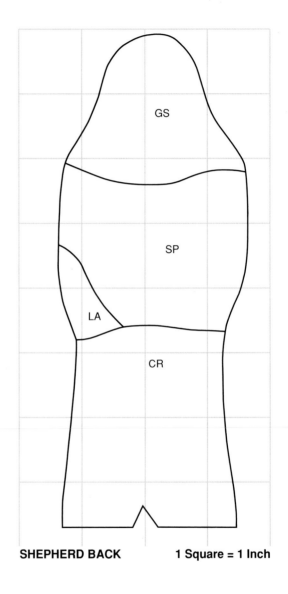

SHEPHERD BACK   **1 Square = 1 Inch**

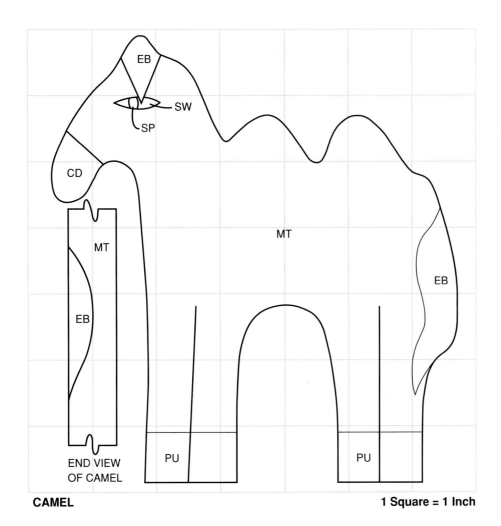

CAMEL

END VIEW
OF CAMEL

1 Square = 1 Inch

continued

AWAY IN A MANGER
continued

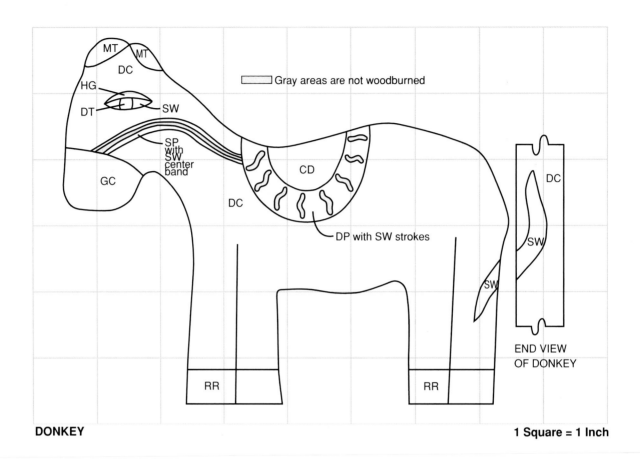

Gray areas are not woodburned

DONKEY

1 Square = 1 Inch

END VIEW
OF DONKEY

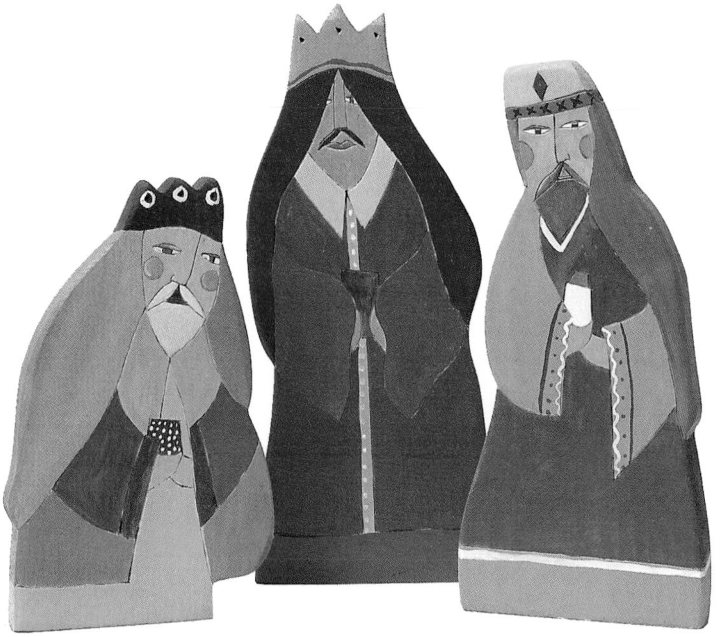

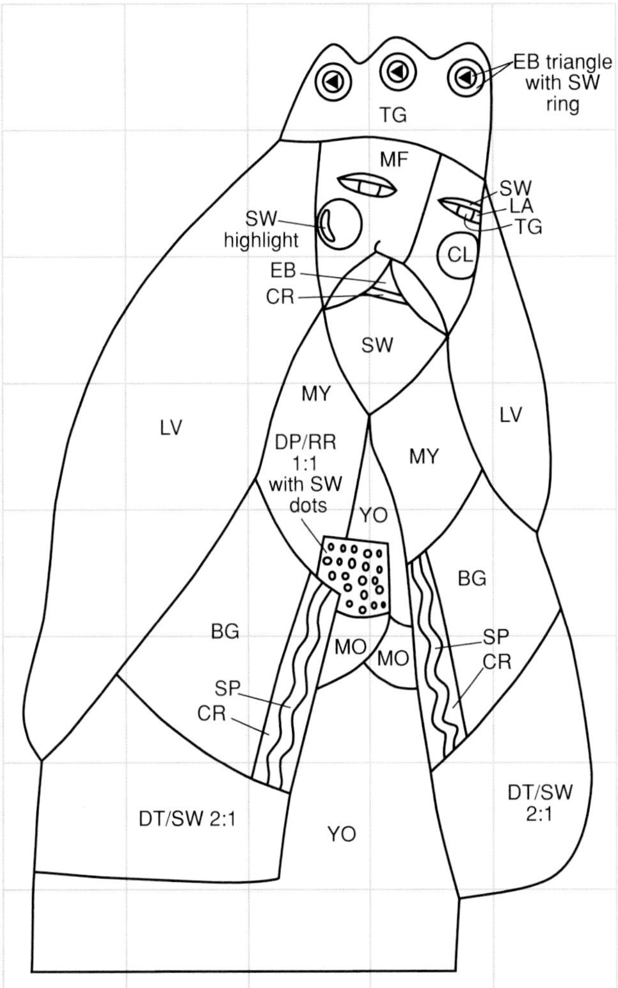
EB triangle
with SW
ring
TG
MF
SW
LA
TG
SW
highlight
CL
EB
CR
SW
MY
LV
LV
DP/RR
1:1
with SW
dots
MY
YO
BG
BG
SP
CR
MO
MO
SP
CR
DT/SW 2:1
YO
DT/SW
2:1

WISE MAN 1 FRONT **1 Square = 1 Inch**

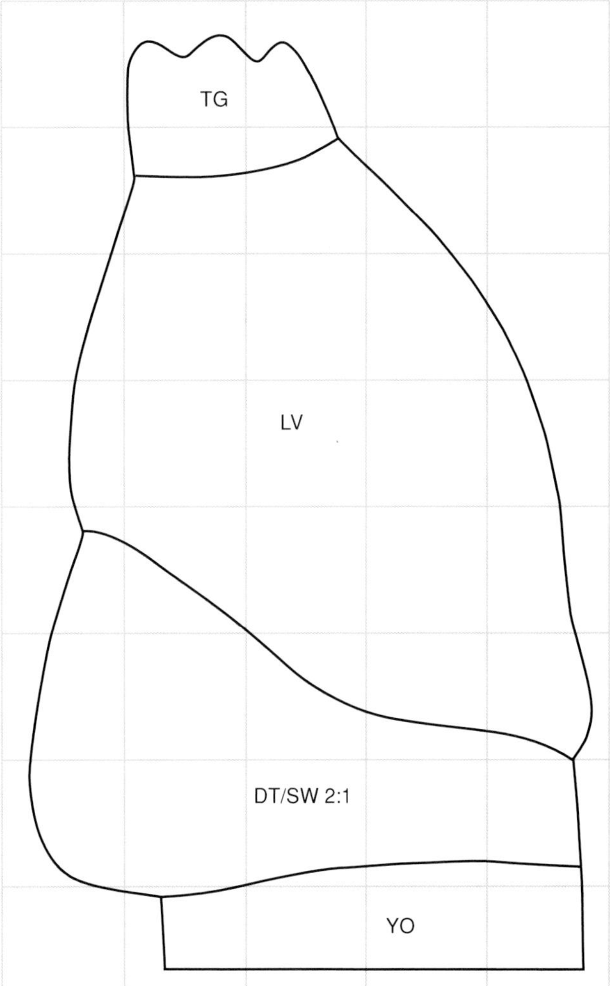
TG
LV
DT/SW 2:1
YO

WISE MAN 1 BACK **1 Square = 1 Inch**

continued

AWAY IN A MANGER
continued

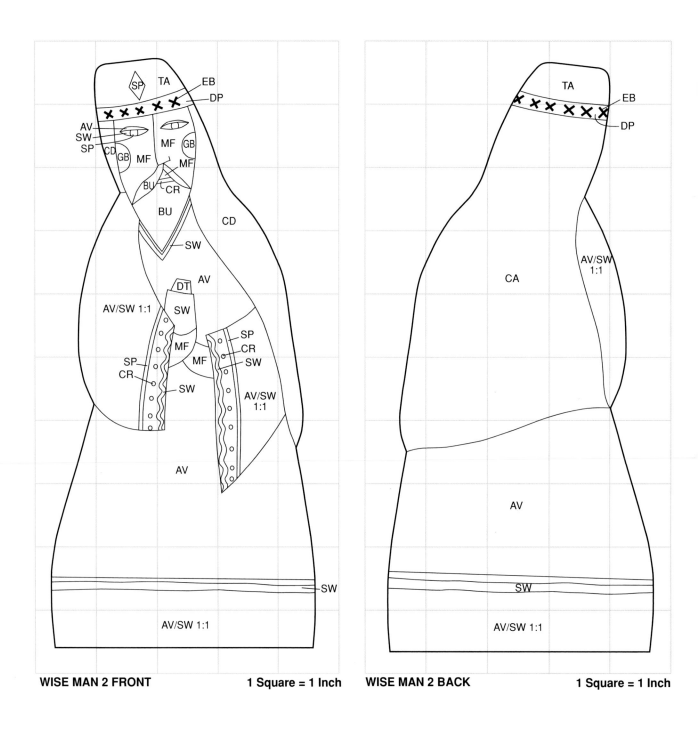

WISE MAN 2 FRONT   1 Square = 1 Inch   **WISE MAN 2 BACK**   1 Square = 1 Inch

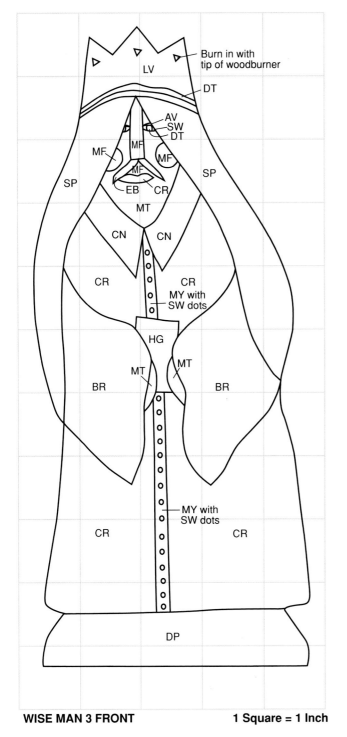

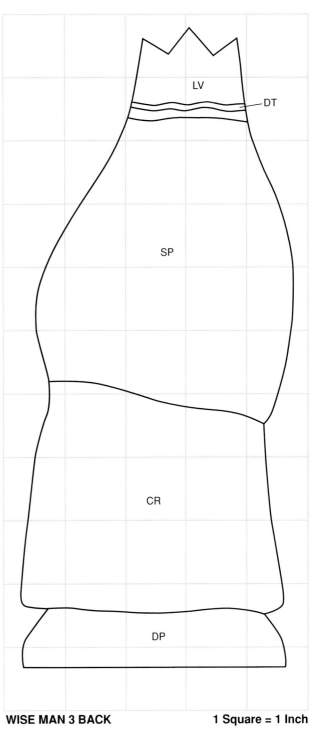

WISE MAN 3 FRONT 1 Square = 1 Inch

WISE MAN 3 BACK 1 Square = 1 Inch

QUICK-AS-
A-WINK GIFTS

You can forget last-minute department-store crowds with this great group of gift ideas. Designed to get you in and out of your shop in a hurry, these projects will make you the most popular Santa on the block.

BUD VASES WITH FLAIR!

Eye-catching curves combine with glass tubes to make these bud vases striking accents for any spot in the home. They're just right for Christmas gifts, too. Follow our hints on designing your own versions to create some styles all your own.

For each large vase, start with a hardwood block about 2x2x5¾"

and an 18x150mm test tube. Or, make a small vase from 1x1x2¾" hardwood and a 12x75 mm test tube. (We used turning squares for stock; see the Buying Guide for our test tube source.)

Draw diagonal lines on one end to locate and mark the center of your stock. Then, drill the test tube hole with a brad-point bit mounted in a drill press. For a large vase,

bore a ¾" hole 5¼" deep (you also could use a spade bit). If you're making a small vase, drill a ½" hole, 2⅜" deep. Hold the stock with a handscrew clamp as you drill.

Now, trace the full-sized front and side vase patterns on *page 56* onto your block, or create your own design. For your own design, sketch flowing curves rather than
continued

BUD VASES WITH FLAIR!
continued

straight lines. Draw a slanted top for a lighter look. For stability, make the base larger than the top. Draw your cutting line across the drilled-out part of the block to create glass windows in the sides. With a bandsaw or scrollsaw, cut along the front pattern lines, saving the side pieces you cut off. Put the sides back into place on the block and secure them with masking tape. Then, cut the side pattern lines.

Round over the edges as you sand the vase with a sanding drum

mounted in a drill press. Then, apply a clear oil finish. Slide the test tube into place. Now, just add flowers and water to bring a cheerful touch to any room in your home.

Buying Guide
• **Test tubes.** Set of three large or six small glass test tubes. For current prices, contact Ennis Mountain Woods, RFD 2, Box 222B, Afton, VA 22920. With each order, please enclose an index card or mailing label with your name and address typed or neatly printed on it.

Project Tool List
Bandsaw or scrollsaw
Drill press
  Bits: ½", ¾"
Sanding drum

Note: We built the project using the tools listed. You may be able to substitute other tools or equipment for listed items you don't have. Additional common hand tools and clamps may be required to complete the project.

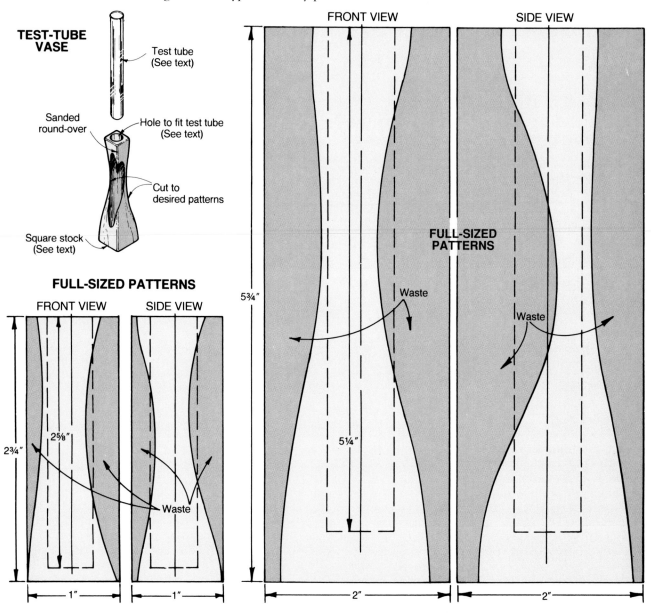

TEST-TUBE VASE
Test tube (See text)
Sanded round-over
Hole to fit test tube (See text)
Cut to desired patterns
Square stock (See text)

FULL-SIZED PATTERNS
FRONT VIEW   SIDE VIEW
2¾"   2⅝"   Waste   1"   1"

FRONT VIEW   SIDE VIEW
FULL-SIZED PATTERNS
5¾"   5¼"   Waste   Waste   2"   2"

CHIMNEY-TOPPED CANDLE HOLDER

There's something about the flicker of candlelight that's so soothing to watch. Provide that relaxed feeling with our smart cherry base and a glass chimney. You'll have a project that's sure to warm someone's heart this holiday season.

1. Cut seven pieces of ¾"-thick stock (we used cherry) to 5×5½" long. Glue and clamp the pieces together face-to-face, with the edges and ends flush.

2. Set your tablesaw blade at 45° from center, and bevel-rip 1" off each of the four corners to make the lamination roughly octagonal in shape. This will make the lamination easier to turn round. Trim both ends of the lamination square (we did this on the radial-arm saw).

3. Screw the lamination to the faceplate (we used a 3" faceplate with ¾" brass wood screws). Position the tool rest in front of the lamination. With the lathe running at about 800 rpm, round down the cherry lamination with a gouge until its diameter measures 4½".

4. Move the tool rest to the end of the candle holder, and form the candle and chimney recesses with a parting tool as shown in the drawing *below*. Check the fit of both the candle and the chimney in their respective recesses for a good fit. (The styles of chimneys vary and are available at most hardware and variety stores, or see the Buying Guide for our source.)

FULL-SIZED HALF PATTERN

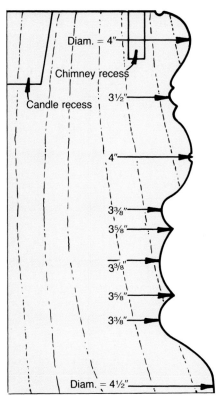

Diam. = 4"

Chimney recess

Candle recess

3½"

4"

3⅜"

3⅝"

3⅜"

3⅝"

3⅜"

Diam. = 4½"

5. Using the full-size half pattern or your own shape, turn the candle holder to shape (we used a ¼" and ½" gouge, a skew, and a parting tool). Allow enough space between the faceplate and the bottom of the holder to avoid hitting the faceplate screws when turning to shape.

6. Using a faster speed (we switched to about 1,500 rpm), finish-sand the candle holder. Slow the lathe to its slowest speed and apply the finish. (We used cherry stain and polyurethane, and placed cardboard behind the lathe to catch the splatter.)

7. Using a parting tool, separate the candle holder from the faceplate as shown in the drawing *below*.

Buying Guide
• **Glass Chimney,** Mushroom lampshade. Catalog No. PO101. For current prices, contact Craft Supplies USA, 1287 East 1120 South, Provo, UT 84601, or call 801-373-0917.

Project Tool List
Tablesaw
Lathe
  3" faceplate
  ¼", ½" spindle gouges
  ¾" skew chisel
  Parting tool

Note: *We built the project using the tools listed. You may be able to substitute other tools or equipment for listed items you don't have. Additional common hand tools and clamps may be required to complete the project.*

HARDWOOD BOOKENDS

Bill of Materials

Part	Finished Size*			Mat.	Qty.
	T	W	L		
A	¾"	4½"	6½"	M	2
B	1¹⁄₁₆"	5"	7¼"	M	2
C	½"	5⅜"	7½"	M	2
D	1¹⁄₁₆"	6"	8½"	M	2
E*	¼"	¼"	¾"	C	4
F*	¼"	¼"	1¹⁄₁₆"	C	8
G*	¼"	¼"	½"	C	4
H*	¼"	¼"	4¼"	C	8
I*	¼"	¼"	4¾"	C	8
J*	¼"	¼"	5¼"	C	8
K*	¼"	¼"	5¾"	C	8
L	¾"	7"	6"	W	2

*Initially cut * parts oversized. Trim them to
finished size according to the instructions.
Material Key: M–mahogany, C–cardinal
wood, W–walnut
Supplies: 6—#8X1½" flathead wood screws,
silicone sealant, four ¼" washers, clear
polyurethane finish.

Cut the books to size and form the dadoes

1. Rip and crosscut the eight books (A, B, C, D) to the sizes listed in the Bill of Materials. (We used different thicknesses of mahogany to make the books.)

2. Raise a ¼" dado blade ¼" above the saw-table surface. Attach an auxiliary wood fence to your miter gauge. Set a stop 1" from the inside edge of the dado blade, and cut dadoes on both surfaces and one edge of the A books. Repeat on the opposite end of book A as shown in the photo *above right*.

3. Using the dimensions on the Exploded View drawing *opposite,* reset the stop and cut ¼" dadoes ¼" deep in books B and D. Lower the blade, reset the stop, and cut ¼" dadoes ⅛" deep in the ½"-thick books C.

Cut and install the blind lines

1. Cut a piece of ¼" cardinal wood to 4X32" for the blind lines

Cut ¼" dadoes in each book blank to house the blind lines.

(E thru K). (We cut a piece of ¾" stock to 4X32" and then resawed it in half on the tablesaw. Next, we planed and sanded one section until its thickness equaled the width of the dadoes in the books.) The extra width of the 4" wide piece makes it easier and safer when ripping the thin strips to width in the next step.

2. Rip seven ¼"-wide strips from the ¼" stock. (After cutting the first

strip on the bandsaw, we checked the fit of the strip in a dado. Then, we adjusted the fence so the strips protruded about ¹⁄₃₂".)

3. Cut the short edge strips (E, F, G) to length plus ¹⁄₁₆". (We used a miter box and backsaw; we feel the pieces are too short to cut safely with power tools.)

4. Center and glue the short strips in place in the dadoes. Hold the pieces in place with masking tape.

5. Cut the blind lines (H, I, J, K) to length plus ¹⁄₁₆". Glue and tape the pieces in place. Sand the strips flush. Due to the shallow dadoes, books C require more sanding.

Here's how to shape the spine

1. Follow the drawing *opposite* to rout the spine edge in each book. Sand the routed edge to the shape shown on the Spine detail.

2. With the back edges and bottoms flush, glue and clamp together four books for each bookend.

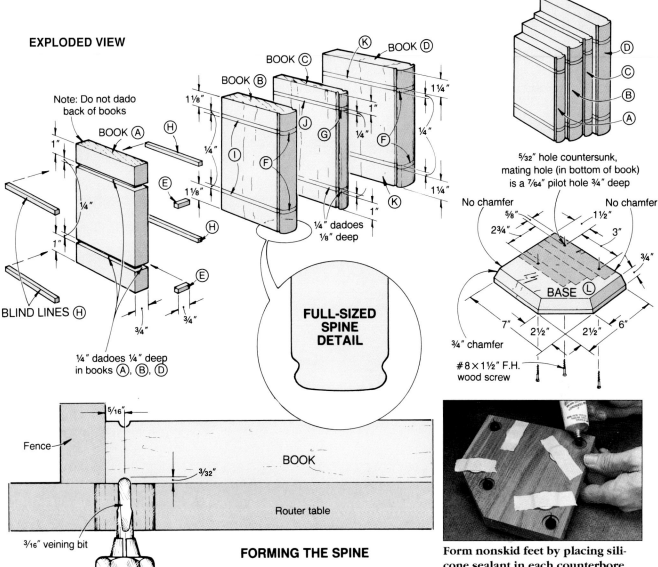

EXPLODED VIEW

Note: Do not dado back of books

BOOK Ⓐ Ⓗ

BOOK Ⓑ

BOOK Ⓒ Ⓚ

BOOK Ⓓ

1"

1⅛"

Ⓔ

1⅛"

¼"

Ⓘ Ⓕ

Ⓙ Ⓖ

¼"

Ⓕ

1"

1¼"

1¼"

¼"

Ⓕ

1"

1¼"

¼" dadoes ⅛" deep

Ⓚ

BLIND LINES Ⓗ

¾"

¾"

¼" dadoes ¼" deep in books Ⓐ, Ⓑ, Ⓓ

BOOK Ⓓ
Ⓒ
Ⓑ
Ⓐ

5/32" hole countersunk, mating hole (in bottom of book) is a 7/64" pilot hole ¾" deep

No chamfer   No chamfer

5/8"   1½"

2¾"   3"

¾"

BASE Ⓛ

7"   2½"   2½"   6"

¾" chamfer

#8 × 1½" F.H. wood screw

FULL-SIZED SPINE DETAIL

5/16"

Fence

3/32"

BOOK

Router table

3/16" veining bit

FORMING THE SPINE

Form nonskid feet by placing silicone sealant in each counterbore.

Add the base and then the finish

1. Cut two pieces of ¾"-thick walnut to 7" wide by 6" long for the bookend bases (L). Mark the angled corner on each base (we used a combination square) as dimensioned on the drawing *above right*. Cut the angled corner.

2. Rout a ¾" chamfer on each walnut base where shown on the drawing *above right*.

3. On the bottom of each base, mark the locations, and then drill three mounting holes. With the back and inside edges flush, clamp the laminated books to the bases. Using the holes in the bases as

guides, drill 7/64" pilot holes ¾" deep into the bottom of the books.

4. To make your own nonskid feet, bore four ¾" holes ⅛" deep in the corners of each base. Put a puddle of silicone sealant in each hole as shown in the photo *above right* (the silicone should protrude about ⅛" above each hole). Tape four ¼" flat washers to the bottom of each base to act as spacers. To flatten the protruding silicone, set each base on a piece of glass or waxed paper until the silicone hardens. Then, fasten the books to the top of each base. Sand smooth and add the finish.

Project Tool List

Tablesaw
    Dado blade or dado set
Router
    Router table
    Bits: 3/16" veining, chamfer
Portable drill
    Bits: 7/64", 5/32", ¾"
Finishing sander

Note: *We built the project using the tools listed. You may be able to substitute other tools or equipment for listed items you don't have. Additional common hand tools and clamps may be required to complete the project.*

ONE WHALE OF A NOTEPAD HOLDER

Start with the notepad box

Note: You'll need thin stock for this project. You can resaw or plane thicker stock to ¼" thick.

1. To form the box top and bottom (A), cut a piece of ¼" oak to 4⅞" wide by 14" long. (We planed down a ½"-thick oak board.) Draw a perpendicular line across the board 6½" from one end; then mark the center of the line. Bore a 1" hole at the centerpoint.

2. Cut the ¼" board in two as shown in the photo *above right.* (We set a stop 6½" from the inside edge of the saw blade when cutting the top to length.) Save the 6½"-long oak piece for the box top. From the remaining piece, crosscut the ¼"-thick oak box bottom to a 6½" finished length.

Cut the oak piece in two to form the box top.

3. Locate and drill the ⅛" hole for the pen funnel in the ¼"-thick oak box top.

4. Cut a ¼"-wide by 18"-long strip from the edge of a ½"-thick oak board. Now, cut the box sides (B) and end (C) to length from the 18" strip.

5. With the outside edges flush, glue and clamp the sides and end to the bottom piece. Later, glue and clamp the box top to the bottom assembly.

6. Sand the box smooth. Now, with a table-mounted router and fence, rout ¼" round-overs on the top and bottom edges except at the finger notch. Finish-sand the routed box.

Forming the whale

1. From ¼"-thick walnut, oak, and cherry, cut three pieces 4x4½" long.

2. Cover one face of the oak and one face of the walnut with double-faced tape. Now, stack the three pieces together as shown on the drawing *opposite.* Using carbon paper, transfer the full-sized whale pattern to a 4x4½" piece of paper. Adhere the pattern to the oak with spray adhesive.

3. With a scrollsaw or a bandsaw fitted with a ⅛" blade, cut the whale pieces to shape. Separate the pieces, and remove the tape.

4. Epoxy together all the parts for one whale, except for the pectoral and tail fins. Sand round-overs on the whale body where shown on the Full-Sized pattern.

5. Tape waxed paper to a piece of plywood, and hold the whale body to the plywood with a few small nails. Then, sand a round-over on the front edge of the

Epoxy the pectoral fin to the sanded whale body.

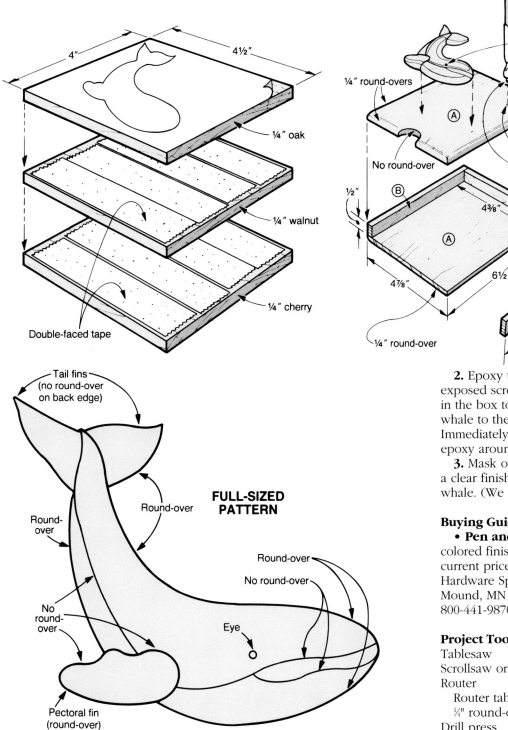

FULL-SIZED PATTERN

Tail fins
(no round-over
on back edge)

Round-over

Round-over

Round-over

No round-over

No
round-over

Round-over

No round-over

Eye

Pectoral fin
(round-over)

¼" oak

¼" walnut

¼" cherry

Double-faced tape

⅛" hole ⅛" deep

Pen and funnel

¼" round-overs

No round-over

1¼"

1¼"

⅛" hole

¼" of thread exposed

Ⓐ

Ⓑ

Ⓒ

Ⓐ

½"

4⅜"

4⅞"

6½"

6½"

Ⓑ

¼"

½"

¼" round-over

pectoral fin, and epoxy it to the whale body where shown in the photo *opposite*. Now, sand the tail fins to shape and epoxy them to the whale body. Later, finish-sand the fins to shape. (We drum-sanded the bottom side of the tail so it wouldn't lie flat on the box.) Locate and drill a ⅛" hole for the eye.

Final assembly

1. Thread the mounting screw into the bottom of the pen funnel. Using a hacksaw, cut the screw so only ¼" of thread protrudes from the bottom of the funnel.

2. Epoxy the funnel with the exposed screw thread into the hole in the box top. Now, epoxy the whale to the top of the oak box. Immediately wipe off any excess epoxy around the whale.

3. Mask off the funnel, and apply a clear finish to the oak box and whale. (We used an aerosol finish.)

Buying Guide

• **Pen and funnel set.** Gold-colored finish. Stock No. 6521. For current prices, contact Meisel Hardware Specialties, P.O. Box 70, Mound, MN 55364-0700, or call 800-441-9870.

Project Tool List
Tablesaw
Scrollsaw or bandsaw
Router
    Router table
    ¼" round-over bit
Drill press
    Bits: ⅛", 1"
    Sanding drum
Finishing sander

Note: *We built the project using the tools listed. You may be able to substitute other tools or equipment for listed items you don't have. Additional common hand tools and clamps may be required to complete the project.*

THE THREE RACK-A-TIERS

I t's time for those tapes and discs to come out from behind the couch and under the coffee table. Here's a trio of simple solutions to keep your collection organized and tastefully displayed. Stack one rack on top of the other to increase your storage space as your collection grows. Or, if you're just starting out, build a single organizer now and construct more as you need them.

Note: The following instructions are for the video rack shown above. *To build the cassette or compact-*

disc rack, refer to the drawings for each and to the note concerning the hole locations on the drawings.

1. From ¾"-thick stock (we used walnut), cut the rack ends to 6" wide by 8¼" long. When cutting the

ends to size, note the grain direction shown in the photo *above.*

2. Mark the hole centerpoints on the inside face of each endpiece (We put the surface with the nicest grain pattern on the outside.) An

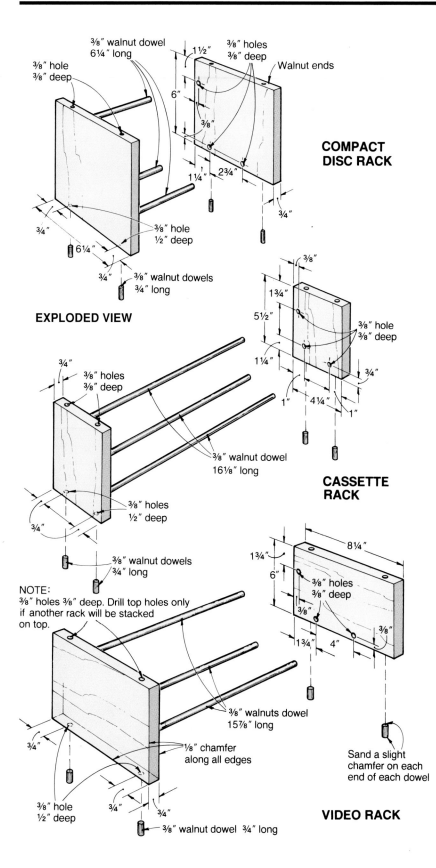

COMPACT DISC RACK

3/8" walnut dowel 6¼" long

3/8" hole 3/8" deep

3/8" holes 3/8" deep

Walnut ends

1½"

6"

3/8"

1¼"   2¾"

¾"

¾"

6¼"

¾"

3/8" hole ½" deep

3/8" hole ¾"

3/8" walnut dowels ¾" long

EXPLODED VIEW

3/8"

1¾"

5½"

1¼"

3/8" hole 3/8" deep

¾"

1"   4¼"   1"

CASSETTE RACK

¾"

3/8" holes 3/8" deep

3/8" walnut dowel 16⅛" long

3/8" holes ½" deep

¾"

3/8" walnut dowels ¾" long

NOTE:
3/8" holes 3/8" deep. Drill top holes only if another rack will be stacked on top.

8¼"

1¾"

6"

3/8" holes 3/8" deep

3/8"

1¾"   4"   3/8"

3/8" walnuts dowel 15⅞" long

⅛" chamfer along all edges

Sand a slight chamfer on each end of each dowel

¾"

3/8" hole ½" deep

¾"   ¾"

3/8" walnut dowel ¾" long

VIDEO RACK

easy way to ensure your holes align is to mark and drill the holes in one endpiece, and then use dowel centers to transfer the hole locations to the other endpiece.

3. If you plan to stack the units as shown *opposite*, mark the hole locations on the top and bottom edges where dimensioned on the drawing. Don't drill holes in the top edge of the uppermost unit. Rout or sand a ⅛" chamfer along all edges.

4. Drill ⅜" holes ⅜" deep at each marked centerpoint on the inside faces and ½" deep in the bottom and top edges where marked.

5. Using a stop for consistent lengths, cut three pieces of ⅜" walnut dowel to length for each rack. Sand a chamfer on each end of each dowel. Glue the dowel between the endpieces. (To avoid wobble in the finished rack, we clamped the endpieces to a flat surface so the bottom edges were level with each other.)

6. Cut ¾"-long pieces of ⅜" dowel for the connecting dowels and feet. Sand a chamfer on both ends of each dowel. Glue the dowels into the bottom edge (they slide into the holes in the top edge of the mating endpiece). Apply a clear finish.

Project Tool List
Tablesaw
Drill press
    ⅜" bit
Router
    Router table
    Chamfer bit
Finishing sander

Note: *We built the project using the tools listed. You may be able to substitute other tools or equipment for listed items you don't have. Additional common hand tools and clamps may be required to complete the project.*

THE END-GRAIN CUTTING BOARD

Simple-to-cut grooves and rabbets add a crafty patterned effect to this laminated board. Similar in construction to a butcher's table, our cutting board will be around for years and years of cutting, dicing, and mincing.

1. From ¾"-thick stock, rip and crosscut four strips of oak and one strip of a darker-colored hardwood (we used cardinal wood; walnut would also work) to 1½" wide by 24" long. Cut a fifth oak strip to 1¼" wide by 24" long.

2. Attach an auxiliary fence and a ¼" dado blade to your tablesaw. Follow Step 1 of the drawing *below left* to cut ¼" grooves ¼" deep *centered* along one edge of all the strips except *one* of the 1½"-wide oak strips. (We cut the grooves in this step and rabbets in the next in scrap stock to ensure gap-free mating joints.)

3. Put the 1¼"-wide oak strip aside. Now, switch to a ½" dado blade and use Step 2 of the drawing as a reference to cut a pair of ¼" rabbets ¼" deep along the opposite edge of the five 1½"-wide strips.

4. Spread glue on the mating edges of the six strips (we used yellow woodworker's glue). Clamp the strips, alternating the direction of the grain, in the configuration shown on Step 3 and accompanying End Grain detail. For ease in gluing and clamping the individual slabs later, check that the lamination is flat; reclamp if necessary. Leave the strips clamped overnight.

5. Remove the clamps and scrape off the excess glue. Carefully belt-sand or scrape both surfaces flat.

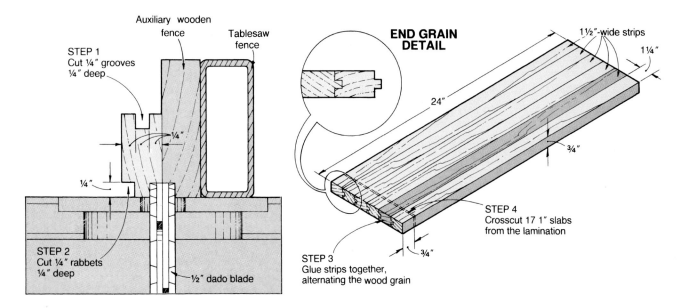

STEP 1
Cut ¼" grooves ¼" deep

Auxiliary wooden fence

Tablesaw fence

¼"

¼"

STEP 2
Cut ¼" rabbets ¼" deep

½" dado blade

END GRAIN DETAIL

1½"-wide strips

1¼"

24"

¾"

STEP 4
Crosscut 17 1" slabs from the lamination

STEP 3
Glue strips together, alternating the wood grain

¾"

Clamp a scrap block to your rip fence for use as a stop to ensure equal-length pieces. The guard was removed for photo clarity.

(We used the edge of a framing square to check for flatness.)

6. Crosscut the lamination into 17 1"-long slabs where shown in Step 4 of the drawing. (As shown in the photo *above*, we clamped a stop to our tablesaw fence, and then positioned the inside edge of the blade 1" from the outside surface of the stop.)

7. Position the pieces next to each other in the order they were cut. Then, flip every other piece to obtain the V-shaped grain configuration shown on Step 5 of the drawing and the project photo.

8. With the surfaces and ends flush, glue and clamp the slabs with the end grain facing up (we used bar clamps). Again, let the

lamination sit overnight before removing the clamps.

9. Sand the cutting board smooth and apply the finish. (We used Behlen's Salad Bowl Finish; a vegetable oil or mineral oil also would work, but we found that several coats of Behlen's completely fills the open-grained oak.)

Buying Guide
• **Behlen's Salad Bowl Finish.**
Safe for wooden bowls, plates, and eating utensils. For current prices, contact Armor Products, Box 445, East Northport, NY 11731, or call 800-292-8296 or 516-462-6228.

Project Tool List
Tablesaw
    Dado blade or dado set
Belt sander
Finishing sander

Note: *We built the project using the tools listed. You may be able to substitute other tools or equipment for listed items you don't have. Additional common hand tools and clamps may be required to complete the project.*

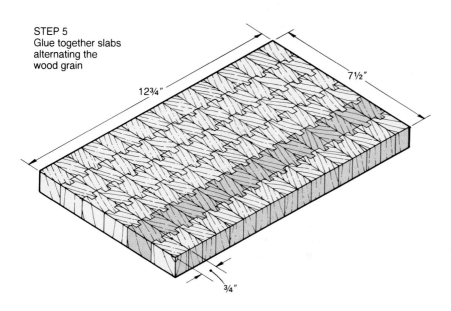

STEP 5
Glue together slabs
alternating the
wood grain

12¾"

7½"

¾"

ONE-OF-A-KIND TREASURES

Here is a group of projects destined to produce future heir-looms. Perfect for giving during the holidays or at any time of year—these are gifts that will be cherished.

JEWEL OF A CASE

Daryl Morgan, a woodworker from Waterloo, Iowa, studied plenty of jewelry boxes before designing this one. "I saw lots of pretty boxes with little emphasis on function," Daryl said. "When designing my box, I incorporated simple Scandinavian-style lines, and then added two sliding trays to make the best of the available space." Well, Daryl, all the ladies we've talked to like what you've accomplished. Thanks for the great design.

Note: You will need thin oak for this project. You can resaw or plane thicker stock to size.

Eight splines make for a sturdy box

1. Cut a piece of ½"-thick oak to 3½" wide by 42" long for the front, back, and ends. Cut a ¼" rabbet ¼" deep along one edge.

2. Square your miter gauge to your saw blade, and then tilt the blade 45° from vertical. Cut scrap to verify the angle setting. Now,

miter-cut the front and back (A) and ends (B) to the lengths listed in the Bill of Materials from the 42"-long piece.

3. Sand the inside face of each piece (A, B). Next, glue and clamp together the pieces, checking for square and making sure that the top and bottom edges remain flush.

4. Using the drawing at *right* as a guide, build a V-block jig. Now, raise the tablesaw blade 1½" above the surface of the saw table. Position the fence 1" from the inside edge of the saw blade and cut a pair of slots in each corner of the mitered box as shown in the photo at *right*.

5. To form the splines, cut a piece of ⅛" stock (we resawed thicker stock) to ¾" wide by 22" long. Then, crosscut twelve 1½"- long splines from the stock. Glue a spline into each slot in the box. After the glue dries, trim the splines (we used a dovetail saw) ¹⁄₁₆" from the surfaces of the box and then sand the splines flush. (You'll use the four remaining splines when forming the lid.)

Now, add the box bottom and tray supports

1. From ⅛" hardboard, measure the opening and cut the bottom (C) to size less ¹⁄₁₆" in each direction. Temporarily tape the bottom into the rabbeted opening.

2. Cut the tray supports (D, E) to size. (We resawed thicker stock to ¼" thick.) Glue the top tray supports (D) to the box front and back, but not the bottom (C). The taped-in-place hardboard will keep the bottom of the tray support flush with the top edge of the ¼" rabbet. Remove the bottom as soon as you
continued

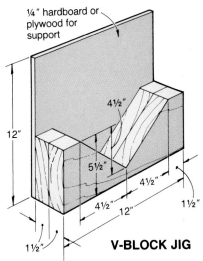

V-BLOCK JIG

¼" hardboard or plywood for support

12"

4½"

5½"

4½"

4½"

12"

1½"

1½"

Using the V-block jig shown in the drawing *above* for support, cut a pair of spline slots in each corner of the box.

JEWEL OF A CASE
continued

Bill of Materials					
Parts	**Finished Size***			**Mat.**	**Qty.**
	T	**W**	**L**		
BOX AND DRAWER SUPPORTS					
A* front & back	½"	3½"	11"	O	2
B* ends	½"	3½"	8½"	O	2
C bottom	⅛"	8"	10½"	H	1
D top dwr. support	¼"	2¼"	10"	O	2
E btm dwr. support	¼"	1¼"	10"	O	2
LID					
F* front & back	½"	2"	11"	O	2
G* ends	½"	2"	8½"	O	2
H* panel	¼"	5$\frac{15}{16}$"	8$\frac{7}{16}$"	EO	1
TRAYS					
I ends	¼"	⅞"	4¼"	O	4
J front & back	¼"	⅞"	7$\frac{7}{16}$"	O	2
K bottom	⅛"	4¼"	7$\frac{3}{16}$"	H	1
L divider	⅛"	⅝"	4"	O	5
M divider	⅛"	⅝"	6$\frac{15}{16}$"	O	1
N front & back	¼"	⅞"	6$\frac{15}{16}$"	O	2
O bottom	⅛"	4¼"	6$\frac{11}{16}$"	H	1
P divider	⅛"	⅝"	3⅞"	O	1

Parts marked with an * are cut larger initially, and then trimmed to finished size. Please read the instructions before cutting.

Material Key: O–oak, EO–edge-joined oak, H–hardboard

Supplies: ¾X1" brass broad hinges (Stanley CD5302), #17 X ½" finish nails, velour fabric, spray-on adhesive or carpet tape, necklace chain, 2—⅜" brass brads, stain, finish.

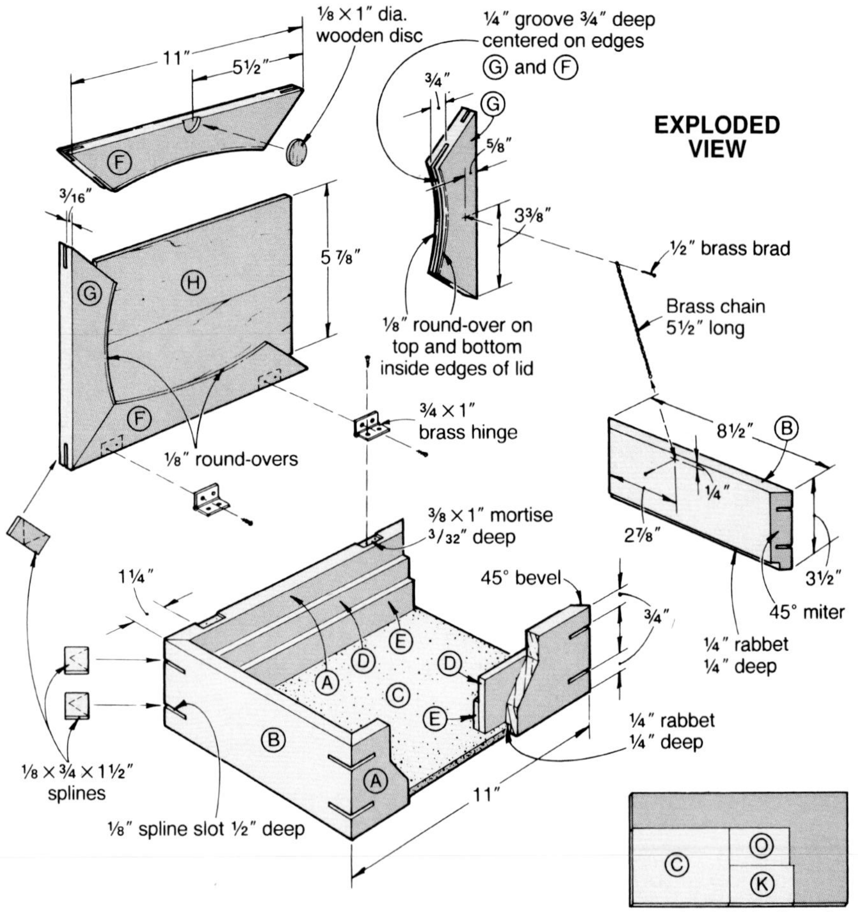
EXPLODED VIEW
⅛ × 1" dia. wooden disc
¼" groove ¾" deep centered on edges G and F
11"
5½"
¾"
⅝"
3⅜"
3/16"
5 ⅞"
½" brass brad
Brass chain 5½" long
⅛" round-over on top and bottom inside edges of lid
¾ × 1" brass hinge
⅛" round-overs
⅜ × 1" mortise 3/32" deep
8½"
¼"
2⅞"
3½"
45° miter
1¼"
45° bevel
¾"
¼" rabbet ¼" deep
¼" rabbet ¼" deep
⅛ × ¾ × 1½" splines
⅛" spline slot ½" deep
11"
⅛ × 12 × 24" Hardboard

CUTTING DIAGRAM
*Plane or resaw to thickness stated in Bill of Materials

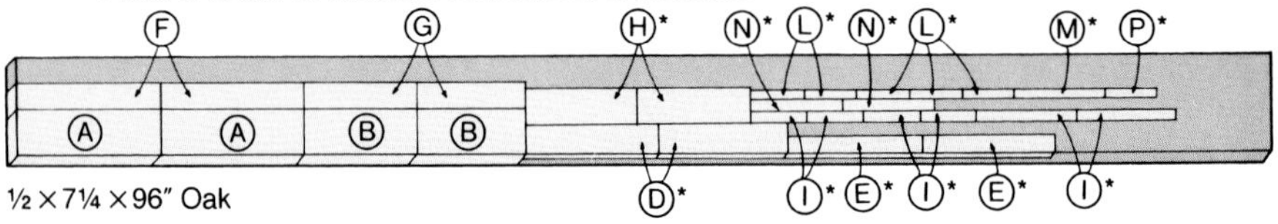
½ × 7¼ × 96" Oak

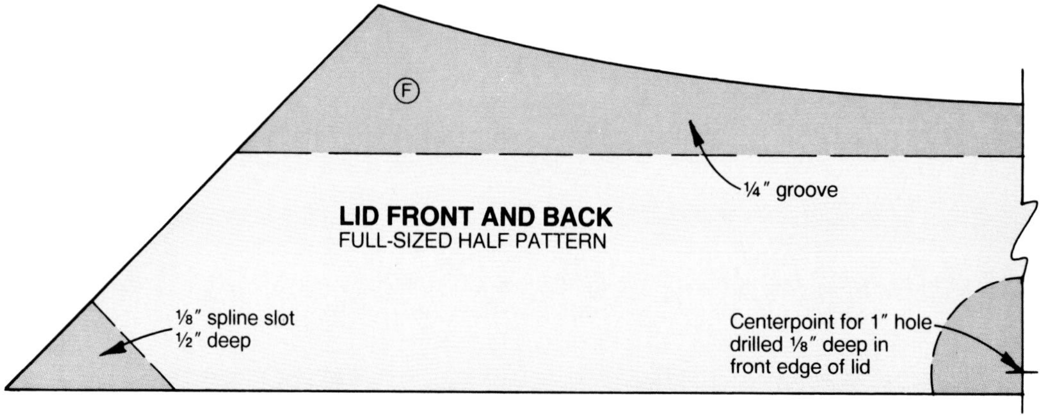
LID FRONT AND BACK
FULL-SIZED HALF PATTERN
¼" groove
⅛" spline slot ½" deep
Centerpoint for 1" hole drilled ⅛" deep in front edge of lid

clamp the supports in place. After the glue dries, repeat the process with the lower tray supports (E).

Next, build the lid

1. Cut a piece of ½" stock to 2x42". Miter-cut the lid front, back, and ends (F, G) to length.

2. Transfer the curve patterns to the top inside surface of each lid piece. Bandsaw the curves smooth. Sand the bandsawed edge to remove the saw marks.

3. Rout or sand ⅛" round-overs along the top and bottom inside curved edge of each lid piece.

4. Fit your tablesaw with a ¼" dado blade. Now, position the fence so the dado blade will cut a ¼" rabbet centered along the curved edge of each lid piece.

5. With double-faced (carpet) tape, adhere a piece of thin hardboard or plywood to your saw top and butted against the fence. Start the saw, and raise the dado blade ¾" above the surface of the hardboard. The hardboard acts as a zero-clearance insert and keeps the bottom edge of the lid parts from falling into the slot around the blade as they would with a standard blade insert. The insert also allows you to smoothly push the lid pieces over the blade.

6. As shown in the photo *above right,* cut a ¼" groove ¾" deep centered along the inside (curved) edge of each lid piece (F, G). (We used a feather board to keep the pieces firmly against the fence when cutting the groove.)

7. For the lid panel (H), resaw or plane thicker stock for two

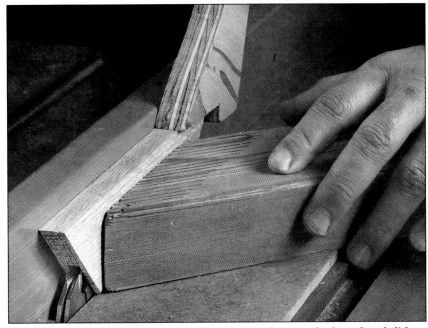

Cut a ¼" groove ¾" deep centered along the inside-curved edge of each lid piece. Use a push stick to feed the stock.

¼"-thick pieces 3x9". Glue the two pieces edge to edge. Now, trim the panel to 5¹⁵⁄₁₆x8⁷⁄₁₆" long. The panel should fit slightly loose in the assembled lid, allowing it to expand without splitting the mitered lid joints.

8. Check the fit, and then glue and clamp the lid pieces, allowing the panel to float (no glue) in the grooved opening.

9. Using the spline jig, cut a ⅛" spline slot ½" deep centered in each corner of the lid. Using the splines cut earlier, glue them in place; trim and sand them flush.

Hinge the lid, and form the finger pull

1. Mark the location and form a pair of ⅜x1" mortises on the top edge of the box back (A). (We cut the mortise outlines with an X-acto knife and removed the waste with a sharp ¼" chisel.)

2. With a Forstner bit, drill a 1" hole ⅛" deep on the bottom side of the lid where shown on the Hole Detail accompanying the Exploded View drawing.

3. Using a plug cutter or bandsaw, cut a 1"-diameter plug from ⅛" stock. Glue the plug into the recess noting the grain direction shown on the Exploded View drawing. Sand the bottom surface flush with the bottom of the lid.

Assemble the two trays

1. Cut the tray pieces (I thru P) to size. Mark the locations and cut ⅛" kerfs in parts L, M, and P where shown on the Tray drawings. (We raised our tablesaw blade ⁵⁄₁₆" above the saw table and used a miter gauge with an auxiliary fence to cut the kerfs.)

2. Cut ¼" rabbets ⅛" deep along the *ends* of parts J and N. Form ³⁄₁₆"
continued

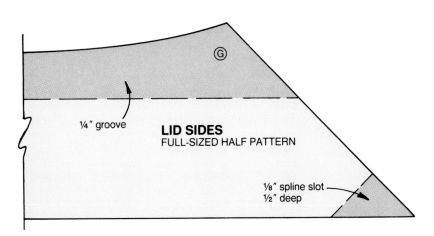

Ⓖ

¼" groove

LID SIDES
FULL-SIZED HALF PATTERN

⅛" spline slot
½" deep

JEWEL OF A CASE
continued

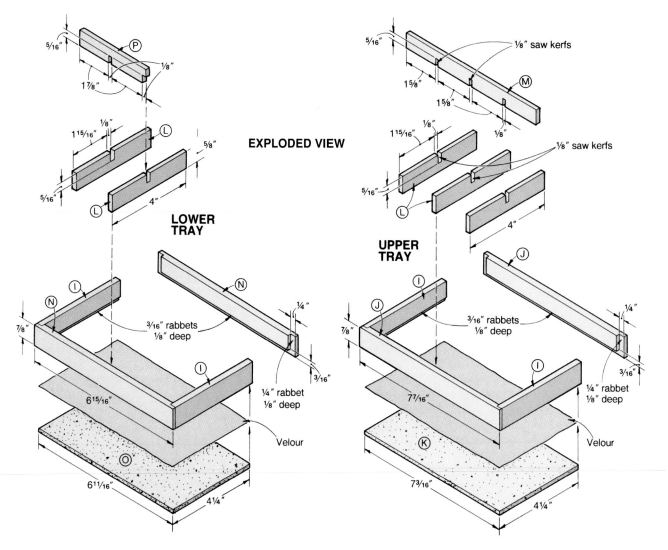

EXPLODED VIEW

LOWER TRAY

UPPER TRAY

⅛" saw kerfs

⅛" saw kerfs

Velour

Velour

3/16" rabbets
⅛" deep

3/16" rabbets
⅛" deep

¼" rabbet
⅛" deep

¼" rabbet
⅛" deep

rabbets ⅛" deep along the *bottom* edge of parts I, J, and N.

3. Cut the tray bottoms (K, O) to size from ⅛" hardboard.

4. Glue each divider assembly (L/M and L/P). Then, glue together each tray, checking for square.

5. Hand-sand the trays and divider assemblies smooth. Glue the dividers in place in each tray.

Apply the finish, and fit the fabric

1. Finish-sand the box, lid, and trays (we sanded with 150- and 220-grit sandpaper). Apply a stain if desired. Add the finish. (We sprayed on several light coats of finish. We found this easier than trying to apply the finish with a brush.)

2. Adhere the velour fabric to the top surface of the box bottom (C) and tray bottoms (K, O). (We applied spray-on adhesive to the top surface of all three parts. You also could use carpet tape.) With an X-acto knife, trim the fabric ends flush with the bottom surface of the hardboard.

3. Secure the box tray bottoms in place. (We held the bottoms in place by running a fine bead of glue along the ends of the hardboard next to the bottom edges of the rabbets.)

4. Fasten the brass hinges to the box, and then screw the hinges to the lid. Add a 5½" length of necklace chain with two brads to the lid and box where shown on the Exploded View drawing.

Project Tool List
Tablesaw
    Dado blade or dado set
Bandsaw
Drill press
    1" Forstner bit
    1" plug cutter
Router
    Router table
    ⅛" round-over bit
Finishing sander

Note: *We built the project using the tools listed. You may be able to substitute other tools or equipment for listed items you don't have. Additional common hand tools and clamps may be required to complete the project.*

ROCKABYE DOLL CRADLE

If you want to be known as the "world's greatest woodworker" at your house, surprise that special someone with this delightful doll cradle for a favorite doll. Our pine beauty measures 24" long and 14" high, and you'll find the work made easy by our full-sized half patterns and detailed assembly instructions.

Start with the frame

1. From ¾" stock (we used pine), rip and crosscut two pieces to 1¾x24¼" for the frame sides (A) of the cradle bottom, and two pieces to 1¾x7¾" for the frame ends of the cradle bottom (B).

(See the Cutting Diagram on *page 74*.) Next, arrange these pieces as shown on the Bed Frame drawing *opposite*, and mark the locations of the two ⅜" dowel holes on the ends of the B pieces as dimensioned.

2. Using a doweling jig and a ⅜" brad-point bit mounted in an electric hand drill, drill the two dowel holes in each end of both B pieces 1¼" deep. Next, drill the mating holes in the side frame members (A) the same way.

3. Crosscut eight pieces of ⅜" dowel to 2⅜" long. Glue a dowel in each of the holes in the ends

of both B pieces. (We used yellow woodworker's glue.) Next, apply glue in the holes in frame members A. Assemble the frame, and clamp with bar clamps to squeeze it gently together. Wipe off any squeeze-out.

4. After the glue dries, remove the clamps. With a ¼" round-over bit in your router, round over all outside edges on the frame. Set the frame aside, but leave the router set up to use later.

continued

ROCKABYE DOLL CRADLE
continued

Make the cradle sides

1. From ¾"-thick pine, rip and crosscut two pieces to 1⅜×22" for the top rails (C). Next, tilt the saw blade 5° from horizontal and bevel-rip two bottom rails (D) to 1⅜" wide. Adjust the blade back to 90° and crosscut the two D pieces to 22". Now, using the same router setup, round over the edges on the rails where shown on the Cradle Side Assembly drawing at *right*.

2. Using the dimensions for the dowel holes on the Cradle Side Assembly drawing, mark the hole locations along the bottom edge of the top rails (C) and along the top edge of the bottom rails (D). (To mark them, we aligned and clamped both pairs of rails together; then, using a square, we measured and scribed lines across their edges.) Chuck a ¼" drill bit in your drill press, clamp a fence to the table ⅜" from the center of the bit, and adjust it to drill a ½"-deep hole in the rails. Place each rail against the fence and drill the holes on the lines.

3. Bevel-sand both ends of each rail piece as shown in the Rail detail accompanying the Cradle Side Assembly drawing. (We used a disc sander.)

4. Next, crosscut 14—¼"-diameter dowels to 5¼" long, and sand a slight taper on the ends of each. Brush a small amount of glue onto the ends of the dowels, insert them in the holes, and assemble both sets of rails as shown *below*. Clamp the assemblies until dry.

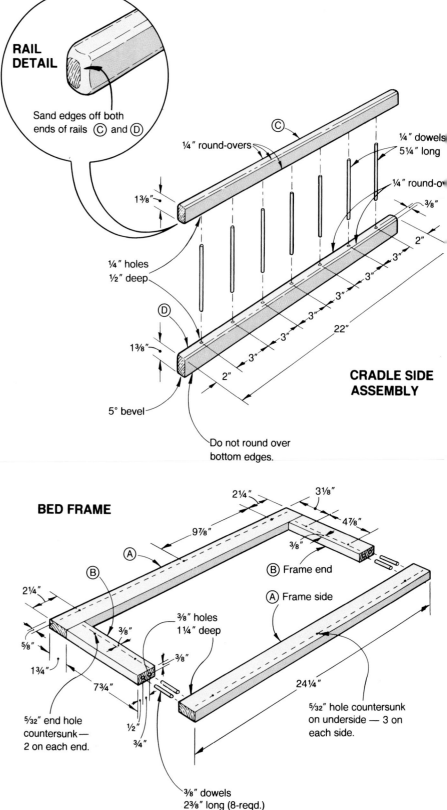

RAIL DETAIL

Sand edges off both ends of rails Ⓒ and Ⓓ

¼" round-overs

1⅜"

¼" holes ½" deep

Ⓓ

1⅜"

2"

5° bevel

Ⓒ

¼" dowels 5¼" long

¼" round-over

⅜"

2"

3"

3"

3"

3"

3"

22"

3"

3"

Do not round over bottom edges.

CRADLE SIDE ASSEMBLY

BED FRAME

2¼"

9⅞"

Ⓐ

Ⓑ

2¼"

⅜"

⅝"

1¾"

7¾"

⅜" holes 1¼" deep

⁵⁄₃₂" end hole countersunk— 2 on each end.

½"

¾"

3⅛"

4⅞"

⅜"

Ⓑ Frame end

Ⓐ Frame side

24¼"

⁵⁄₃₂" hole countersunk on underside — 3 on each side.

⅜" dowels 2⅜" long (8-reqd.)

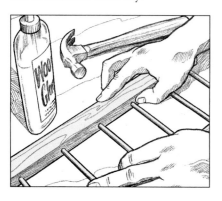

5. To make the posts (E), first rip and crosscut a ¾x¾x36" piece of pine. Using the same router setup described earlier, round over all edges on the piece. Set your saw's miter gauge to 5° from perpendicular with the saw blade, and miter cut the piece into four 9"-long pieces. (The angled ends form the bottoms of the posts.) Now, square the miter gauge to the saw blade, and one by one, crosscut the square ends to attain a final post length of 8½". (We clamped a spacer block to the fence to ensure a uniform length when cutting each piece.) Bevel-sand the top ends of the posts as shown on the Exploded View drawing and Post detail, on *page 74*.

6. Using the dimensions on the Post detail, mark the centerpoints for the four holes on each post. Drill the ⅜" holes ¼" deep. Next, drill ⁵⁄₃₂" holes through the centers of the ⅜" holes, backing the pieces with scrap to prevent chip-out.

7. Orient the angled bottom ends of the posts to match the bevel-cut bottom edges of the bottom rails (D) and align. Attach the posts to the rail ends as shown *below*, drilling ⁷⁄₆₄" pilot holes, and drive #8x1¼" flathead wood screws.

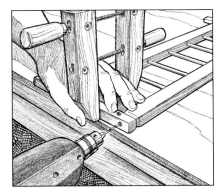

Next, make the headboard, footboard, and rockers

1. To make the headboard (F) and footboard (G), rip and crosscut six 3⅛ x10⅝" pieces of ¾" pine. Edge-join the pieces into two panels of three pieces. Clamp the panels (we used bar clamps) and wipe off any glue squeeze-out. After the glue dries, remove the clamps, and sand.

2. Make a full-sized pattern of the headboard by placing a sheet of tracing paper over the half pattern on *page 75*. Align the left edge of the paper with the centerline, and then trace the outline of the half-headboard pattern onto the paper. Next, remove it and tape a second piece of paper to the left edge of the tracing paper with the half pattern and fold it back under. Cut out the half pattern with scissors, and then unfold it to make a full pattern. Make a pattern of the footboard, using the same technique.

3. Spray adhesive onto the backs of the two patterns, and adhere them to the panels. Bandsaw both pieces to shape. Remove the patterns.

4. Sand the cut edges smooth (we used a 2" drum sander). Next, using the same router setup, round over the top and sides (but not the bottoms) of both pieces. Finish-sand both pieces.

5. Rip and crosscut two ¾"-thick pieces of pine to 4x17". Using double-sided tape, stick the pieces together, face to face, aligning the edges. Make a full-sized pattern of the rocker on *page 75* using the technique described in Step 2. Adhere the pattern to the top piece. Bandsaw the rockers (H) to shape, cutting just outside the line, and sanding to the line. (We used a disc sander to sand the outside curves, and a drum sander on the inside curves.) Separate the rockers and remove the tape. Round over the curved edges where indicated. Sand.

6. For the cradle bottom (I), rip and crosscut a ¼"-thick piece of plywood to 9x22". Finish-sand.

Assemble the cradle

1. Mark one face of the frame to designate it as the bottom side. Next, using the dimensions on the Bed Frame drawing, lay out the six side holes and four end holes. Drill and countersink the holes. (We backed the frame with scrap to prevent chip-out when drilling.)

2. Screw and glue the rockers to the underside of the frame where shown in the End View detail on

the Exploded View drawing on *page 74*, aligning the inside face of the rocker with the inside edge of the frame. (We used #8x2" flathead wood screws.)

3. Attach the cradle sides to the footboard and headboard, using #8x1¼" flathead wood screws. (We used large rubber bands to temporarily hold the parts together. We then checked the assembly with a square, drilled the ½"-deep ⁷⁄₆₄" pilot holes into the head- and footboards, and drove the screws.)

4. Turn the assembly upside down, apply glue to the bottom edge, and center the bed frame and rockers assembly on it. (We had ⅜" relief on each side and ¼" on the ends.) Clamp this assembly in position. (We used two small C-clamps on each side.) Now, drill pilot holes ½" deep through the holes along the frame sides and into the bottom rails of the cradle sides. Drive the #8x1¼" wood screws.

5. Glue the ⅜" screw hole buttons in the screw holes in the posts.

6. Place the plywood bottom you cut earlier into the cradle. Nail it in place with 2d finish nails.

7. Finish-sand, and apply the finish of your choice. (We stained our cradle a medium maple, and then sprayed on two coats of glossy polyurethane, sanding between coats.)

Project Tool List
Tablesaw
Bandsaw
Portable drill
  Doweling jig
Drill press
  Bits: ⁷⁄₆₄", ⁵⁄₃₂", ¼", ⅜"
  2" sanding drum
Router
  Router table
  ¼" round-over bit
Finishing sander

Note: *We built the project using the tools listed. You may be able to substitute other tools or equipment for listed items you don't have. Additional common hand tools and clamps may be required to complete the project.*

continued

ROCKABYE DOLL CRADLE
continued

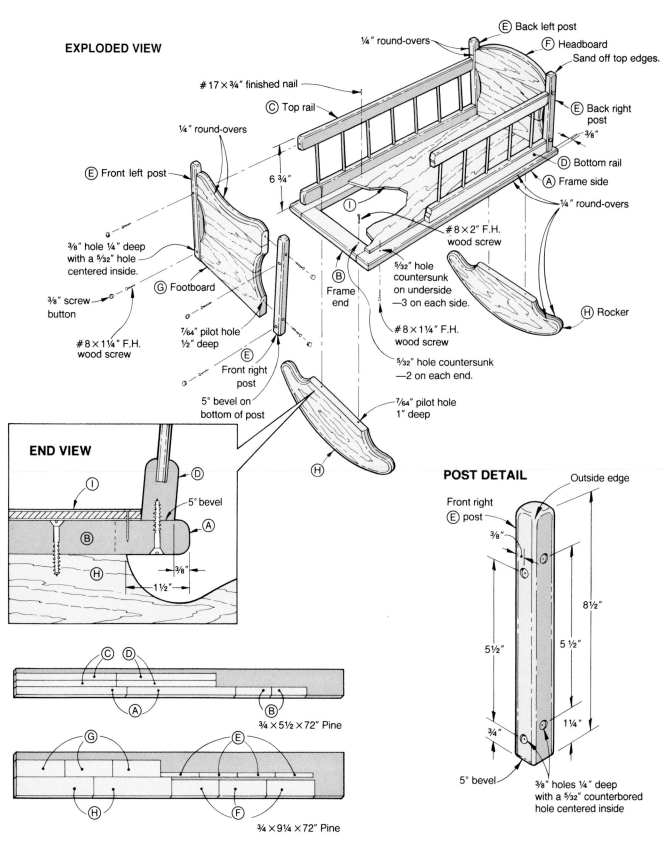

EXPLODED VIEW

E Back left post

¼″ round-overs

F Headboard
Sand off top edges.

#17 × ¾″ finished nail

C Top rail

E Back right post

¼″ round-overs

3/8″

E Front left post

D Bottom rail

A Frame side

6 ¾″

¼″ round-overs

3/8″ hole ¼″ deep
with a 5/32″ hole
centered inside.

I

G Footboard

3/8″ screw
button

B

Frame
end

#8 × 2″ F.H.
wood screw

5/32″ hole
countersunk
on underside
—3 on each side.

H Rocker

7/64″ pilot hole
½″ deep

E

#8 × 1¼″ F.H.
wood screw

#8 × 1¼″ F.H.
wood screw

Front right
post

5/32″ hole countersunk
—2 on each end.

5° bevel on
bottom of post

7/64″ pilot hole
1″ deep

H

END VIEW

I

D

5° bevel

A

B

H

3/8″

1½″

POST DETAIL

Outside edge

Front right
E post

3/8″

8½″

5½″

5 ½″

3/4″

1¼″

3/8″

5° bevel

3/8″ holes ¼″ deep
with a 5/32″ counterbored
hole centered inside

C D

A

B

¾ × 5½ × 72″ Pine

G

E

H

F

¾ × 9¼ × 72″ Pine

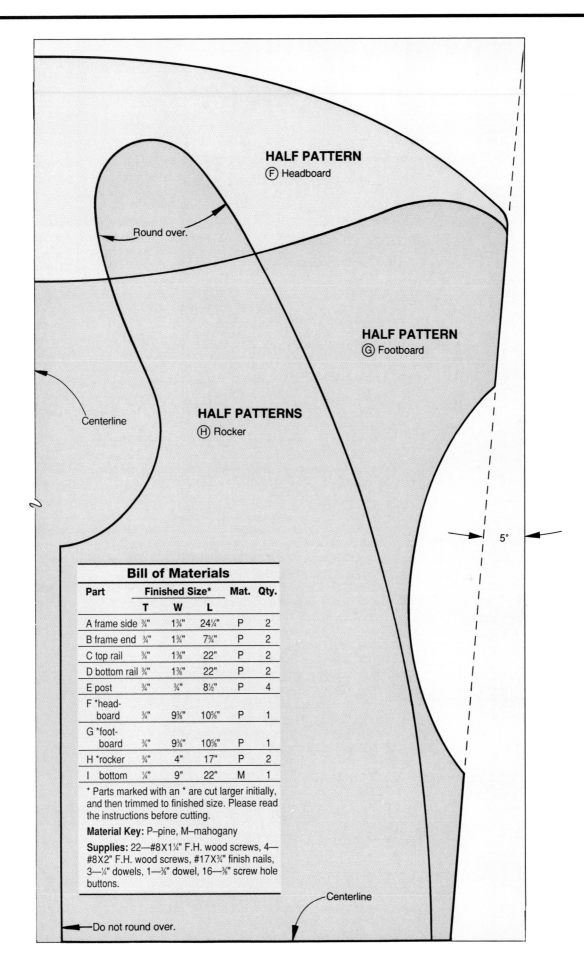

HALF PATTERN
Ⓕ Headboard

Round over.

HALF PATTERN
Ⓖ Footboard

Centerline

HALF PATTERNS
Ⓗ Rocker

5°

Bill of Materials				
Part	Finished Size*		Mat.	Qty.
	T	W	L		
A frame side	¾"	1¾"	24¼"	P	2
B frame end	¾"	1¾"	7¾"	P	2
C top rail	¾"	1⅜"	22"	P	2
D bottom rail	¾"	1⅜"	22"	P	2
E post	¾"	¾"	8½"	P	4
F *head-board	¾"	9⅜"	10⅝"	P	1
G *foot-board	¾"	9⅜"	10⅝"	P	1
H *rocker	¾"	4"	17"	P	2
I bottom	¼"	9"	22"	M	1

* Parts marked with an * are cut larger initially, and then trimmed to finished size. Please read the instructions before cutting.

Material Key: P–pine, M–mahogany

Supplies: 22—#8X1¼" F.H. wood screws, 4—#8X2" F.H. wood screws, #17X¾" finish nails, 3—¼" dowels, 1—⅜" dowel, 16—⅜" screw hole buttons.

Centerline

◄—Do not round over.

HANDWOVEN WHAT-NOT BASKET

Our travels around the country to the nation's top crafts fairs bring us in contact with many beautiful woodworking projects. But on a recent trek to Minnesota, we did a double-take when we happened onto this hardwood basket from designer/woodworker Keith Raivo. It's easy to make, thanks to Keith's method of cutting the weavers with a tablesaw.

Note: You'll need thin stock for this project. You can resaw or plane thicker stock to size.

Preparing the stock

1. For the base (A), uprights (B, C), bottom oak band (D), narrow walnut weavers (E), wide walnut weavers (F), center oak weaver (G), top oak bands (H, I), and lid pieces (J, K), rip and crosscut ¾"-thick, straight-grained boards to the size shown on the Cutting Diagram *below*. The pieces are cut large initially for safety when machining them later.

2. Plane the pieces to the thickness listed on the Cutting Diagram.

Start with the base

1. Using carbon paper or a photocopy and spray-on adhesive, transfer the full-sized Base pattern and the 10 upright locations to the bottom side of the base blank (A).

2. Bandsaw the blank to shape and sand the cut edge smooth. Set the base aside for now.

Rip the thin strips with ease

Note: We cut twice as many bands and weavers (D, E, F, G, H,

CUTTING DIAGRAM

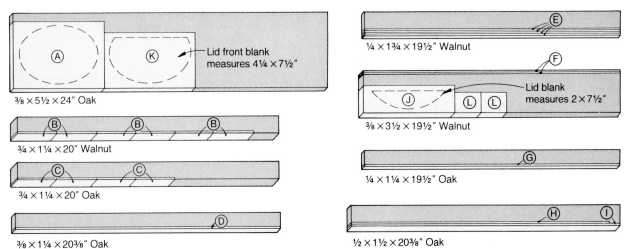

Lid front blank measures 4¼ × 7½"

⅜ × 5½ × 24" Oak

¾ × 1¼ × 20" Walnut

¾ × 1¼ × 20" Oak

⅜ × 1¼ × 20⅜" Oak

¼ × 1¾ × 19½" Walnut

Lid blank measures 2 × 7½"

⅜ × 3½ × 19½" Walnut

¼ × 1¼ × 19½" Oak

½ × 1½ × 20⅜" Oak

I) as needed; it's easy to break the thin strips during construction.

1. Stick a piece of masking tape to the tablesaw top where shown on the Strip Ripping setup drawing. Position a straightedge against both sides of the saw blade and mark blade-reference lines on the masking tape. Now, mark a line parallel to the outside reference line ¹⁄₁₆" away from the blade where shown on the drawing. (To prevent the thin strips from falling into the saw, we cut a piece of hardboard to the same shape and thickness as the tablesaw insert. With the hardboard insert taped in place, we slowly raised the rotating blade through the hardboard to make a zero-clearance insert.)

2. Position the outside edge of the 20"-long walnut upright blank (B) along the ¹⁄₁₆" reference line. Using a push stick, rip a strip from the edge of the walnut. Measure the width of the strip and re-mark the line if the strip doesn't measure ¹⁄₁₆" (it took us a couple of tries).

3. Crosscut six uprights (B) to 3" long from the ¹⁄₁₆"x¾"x20" strip.

4. Repeat the procedure to cut the oak uprights (C), the bottom oak band (D), and the top bands (H, I) to size. Trim the top inside band (I) to length—it's slightly shorter than the top outside band (H).

5. Remove the masking tape, mark a second line ¹⁄₃₂" from the outside blade-reference line, follow the procedure just described to cut ¹⁄₃₂"-thick weavers (E, F, G).

Attach the uprights and start weaving

1. Using instant glue or epoxy, secure the oak and walnut uprights (B, C) to the oak base where previously marked. After you have glued all the uprights in place, sand the bottom of the base to remove the upright-location pencil marks.

continued

Part	Finished Size			Mat.	Qty.
	T	**W**	**L**		
A base	⅜"	4¼"	6"	O	1
B uprights	¹⁄₁₆"	¾"	3"	W	6
C uprights	¹⁄₁₆"	¾"	3"	O	4
D bottom band	¹⁄₁₆"	⅜"	20⅜"	O	1
E narrow weavers	¹⁄₃₂"	¼"	19½"	W	4
F wide weavers	¹⁄₃₂"	⅜"	19½"	W	2
G center weaver	¹⁄₃₂"	¼"	19½"	O	1
H top (in) band	¹⁄₁₆"	½"	18⅞"	O	1
I top (out) band	¹⁄₁₆"	½"	20⅜"	O	1
J lid back	⅜"	1½"	6"	W	1
K lid front	⅜"	3¼"	6½"	O	1
L hinges	⅜"	⅞"	1⁵⁄₁₆"	W	2

Bill of Materials

Material Key: O–oak, W–walnut
Supplies: Instant glue, double-faced tape, masking tape, 1⅛"X½"X6" leather strip, finish.

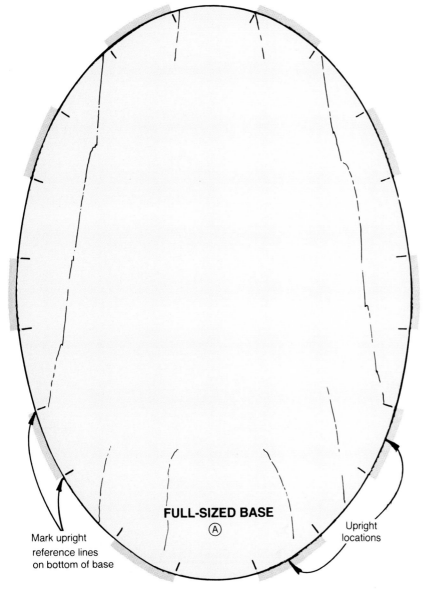

FULL-SIZED BASE
Ⓐ

Mark upright reference lines on bottom of base

Upright locations

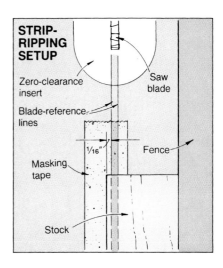

STRIP-RIPPING SETUP

Zero-clearance insert

Saw blade

Blade-reference lines

Masking tape

Fence

¹⁄₁₆"

Stock

HANDWOVEN WHAT-NOT BASKET
continued

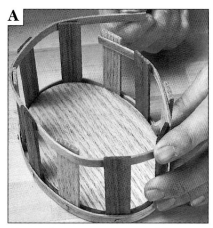

2. Belt-sand a taper on both ends of the bottom band (D) and the top bands (H, I). See the Bottom Band detail *below right* for reference.

3. To make the strips (D, E, F, G, H, I) easier to bend, soak them overnight in water. (We had to weight ours down to keep them from floating to the surface of the cake pan.)

4. Drill pilot holes, and glue and nail the bottom oak band (D) to the basket base. (See the Buying Guide *opposite* for our source of copper clench nails.)

5. As shown in Photo A, weave the bottom walnut weaver (E) through the uprights. (We wove the weaver at the top of the uprights. Once we completed the loop, we slid the weaver down next to the base.) Repeat the process until all but the top two bands (H, I) have been woven into place.

6. Loop the inside oak band (H) into position. Center the outside top band (I) over the *front* walnut upright (B). Clamp the band in place as shown in Photo B. Drill a ¹⁄₁₆" hole through the top bands and upright as shown in the photo.

7. Fit a nail through the hole. Snip the pointed end of the nail with wire cutters so only ¹⁄₁₆"

protrudes on the inside of the basket. Using a ball-peen hammer, rivet (flatten) the nails as shown in Photo C. Repeat the drilling and nailing at each upright, overlapping the bands as shown on the Fastening detail *opposite*. Let the box dry overnight.

To top things off, add the lid

1. Tape the lid back blank (J) to the lid front blank (K) with the surfaces and ends flush. (We used double-faced tape.)

2. Turn the basket upside down, and place it on the taped-together lid pieces so the basket covers 1½" of the walnut lid back.

3. Tape the woven basket to the lid pieces as shown in Photo D. With the lead of a sharp pencil in the hole of a ⁵⁄₁₆" washer, trace around the basket to lay out the shape of the lid as shown in the photo. Cut the lid to shape, and sand the cut edges smooth.

4. Chuck a ⅜" round-over bit in your table-mounted router. Rout a partial round-over on the top edge of the taped-together lid pieces where shown on the Hinge/Round-Over detail *opposite*. Sand smooth, and remove the tape holding the lid pieces together.

Weave the weaver into position at the top of the uprights. Then, slide the weaver against the base.

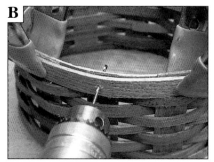

Drill a ¹⁄₁₆" hole through the top outside band, center walnut upright, and top inside oak band.

Use a ball-peen hammer and the top of your vise or an anvil to rivet the nail on the inside of the basket.

Using a washer to ensure an even overhang, transfer the lid outline onto the taped-together lid pieces.

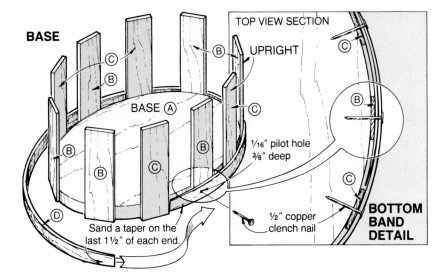

BASE

TOP VIEW SECTION

UPRIGHT

BASE Ⓐ

¹⁄₁₆" pilot hole
⅜" deep

½" copper
clench nail

BOTTOM BAND DETAIL

Sand a taper on the last 1½" of each end.

Forming the hinges and attaching the lid

1. Using the full-sized Hinge Pattern *below right*, lay out two hinges, including the opening and the nail hole centerpoint, on ⅜" walnut stock. Cut the hinges to size. Drill a blade start hole and use a scrollsaw or a coping saw to cut the opening in each hinge to shape.

2. Sand a slight round-over on all top edges of each hinge.

3. Mark the hinge slot locations on the lid back (J) where dimensioned on the Lid Back drawing *below right*. Drill start holes and cut the openings to shape. Sand a slight chamfer on the front and back edges of each opening for a better fit later of the hinge straps. (For reference, see the Hinge/Round-Over detail accompanying the drawing titled Attaching the Lid.)

4. From ⅛"-thick by ½"-wide leather, cut two strips 3" long each. Loop the leather through the hole in each hinge. (We bought our leather at Tandy—you also could get it at a shoe repair store.) With the ends flush, glue together the ends of the leather strips. (We used instant glue and left just enough free play for the hinge to rotate snugly in the leather loop.

5. Wrap a leather strap around a hinge, slip a strap through each slot in the lid back. Drill a ¹⁄₁₆" hole through each leather strap where shown on the Hinge/Round-Over detail. Push a nail through each hole in the leather, and then bend it over as shown on the detail.

6. Hold the lid front (K) ¹⁄₁₆" away from the lid back, and mark the hinge locations on the lid front.

Glue and clamp the hinges to the lid front where marked. Later, remove the clamps, and drill a ¹⁄₁₆" hole through each hinge and lid. Drive a copper clench nail through each hole—these two nails are for appearance only.

Final assembly and presto, it's done!

1. Carefully belt-sand the top of the uprights flush with the top oak bands. Then, hand-sand the entire basket with 220-grit sandpaper. (Soaking the wood causes lots of raised grain.)

2. Glue and clamp the lid back (J) to the basket with an even overhang around the back edge. Immediately wipe off excess glue with a damp cloth.

3. Apply a clear finish. (We used an oil finish; an aerosol also would work well to help cover all those hard-to-get-at places.)

Buying Guide

• **Copper nails.** 100-percent hard-drawn ½"-long copper clench nails, made in England. For current prices, contact Faering Design, Inc., P.O. Box 805, Shelburne, VT 05482. No phone orders please.

Project Tool List

Tablesaw
Bandsaw
Scrollsaw
Stationary belt sander
Router
   Router table
   ⅜" round-over bit
Portable drill
   Bits: ¹⁄₁₆", ⅛"
Finishing sander

Note: We built the project using the tools listed. You may be able to substitute other tools or equipment for listed items you don't have. Additional common hand tools and clamps may be required to complete the project.

Round over top edges

FULL-SIZED HINGE

¹⁄₁₆" hole centerpoint

LID BACK Ⓙ

Hinge slots

5/16"
3/16"

1¼"   ½"   ½"   1¼"

1½"

⅛ × ½ × 3" leather

HINGE Ⓛ

½" copper clench nail

¹⁄₁₆" pilot hole

LID Ⓙ BACK

ATTACHING THE LID

LID FRONT Ⓚ

Sand a slight chamfer on front and back edges

Partial round-over

Ⓗ
Ⓘ

FASTENING DETAIL

Ⓘ
Ⓗ
Ⓑ
Ⓐ
Ⓒ

HINGE/ROUND-OVER DETAIL

¹⁄₁₆"
HINGE
Ⓙ
Ⓛ
Slight chamfer
⅜" round-over bit
½" clench nail
Drill a ¹⁄₁₆" hole below bottom of Ⓙ
Leather hinge strap

¹⁄₁₆" pilot hole

½" copper clench nail
Ⓓ

Ⓔ
Ⓕ Ⓖ

THE CONNOISSEUR'S CRIBBAGE BOARD

Even a busy guy like Santa can't resist playing cribbage on this laminated game board. After you've played the last hand, you can open the sliding door—hidden on the board's bottom side—to conveniently store a deck of cards and the game pegs.

Cut the board pieces to size

1. Cut one piece of 1⅛"-thick maple (¾ stock) to 1¼" wide by 22" long. Later, you'll cut the maple in half to form the two streets (A).

2. Cut a piece of ¾"-thick walnut to 2⅝x10" long for the center strip (B). (We used a piece of highly figured walnut.)

3. From ½" or ¾" walnut stock, cut a piece to 2¹³⁄₁₆x12" for the sliding door (C) and the doorstop (D).

Plane or resaw the piece to ⁵⁄₁₆" thick for parts C and D.

Machine the maple streets

1. Chuck a ½" dovetail bit into your table-mounted router. Position the bit and router table fence where shown on the drawing at *right*. Start the router, and rout along one edge of the 22"-long maple strip.

2. Crosscut two 10" maple streets from the 22"-long strip. With double-faced tape, tape the two 10" strips together side by side with the routed areas facing each other. Now, cut out or make a photocopy of the

full-sized Hole pattern *opposite*. Apply spray adhesive to the back side of the pattern, and stick it to one of the maple streets.

3. Use a try square to mark lines through the hole center points and across the other maple street where shown on the photo *opposite*.

4. Chuck a ⅛" brad-point bit into the drill press. Position the center of the bit directly over one of the center points in the outer row on the pattern. As shown in the photo *opposite*, clamp a fence (we used a straight board) to your drill press table so you can drill all the holes in the outer row in a straight line. Mark a line on the fence directly behind the bit where shown in the photo.

5. Drill ⅛" holes ¼" deep to complete the outer row. (We used the depth stop on our drill press to ensure consistent hole depths.) Without moving the fence, turn the maple lamination end for end and drill the other outer row of holes.

6. Realign the bit with a center point in the inner row, and position the fence. Next, drill the holes for the two inner rows. Separate the streets and remove the tape.

ROUTING THE DOVETAIL RECESS

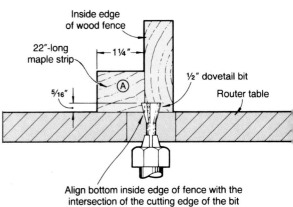

Align bottom inside edge of fence with the intersection of the cutting edge of the bit and the top surface of the router table.

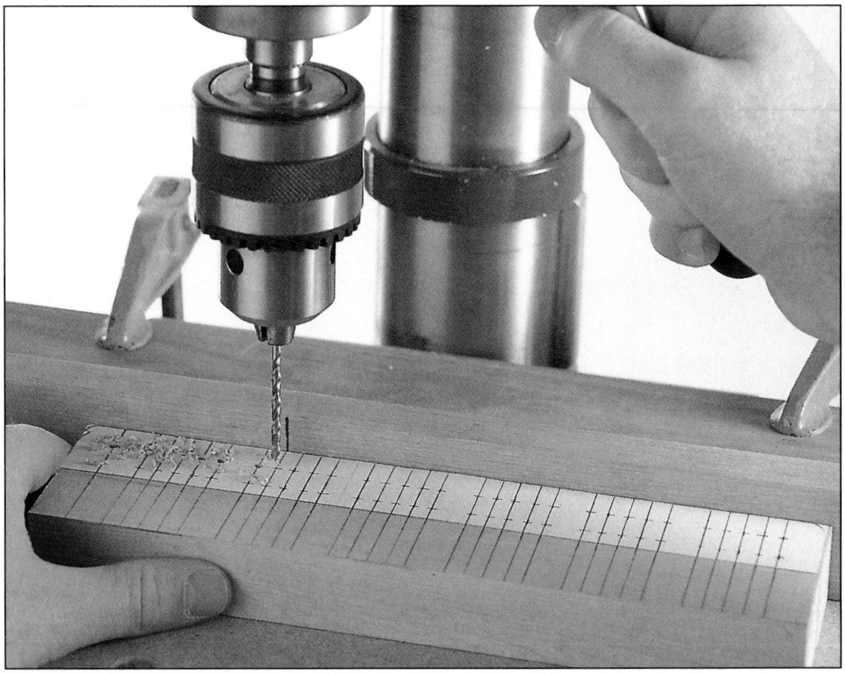

Use the fence and marked lines to drill evenly spaced player holes.

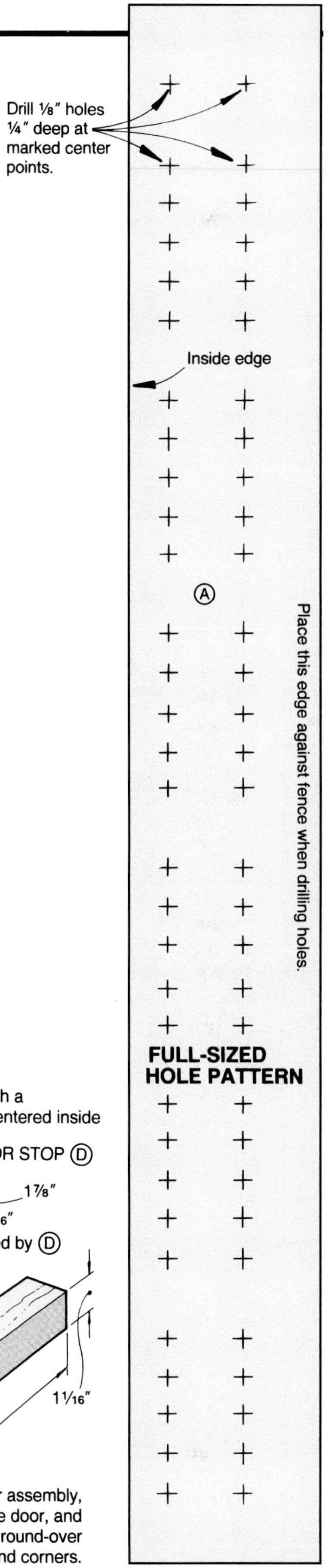
Drill 1/8″ holes 1/4″ deep at marked center points.
Inside edge
Ⓐ
Place this edge against fence when drilling holes.
FULL-SIZED HOLE PATTERN

Now, hollow out the center strip cavities

1. Using the dimensions on the Exploded View drawing *below,* mark the locations, and cut the dadoes for the playing-card and player cavities. Sand the bottoms of the dadoes.

2. Mark the centerpoint, and drill the holes for the bullet catch. (See the hole sizes on the Exploded View drawing and accompanying Catch detail.)

continued

Bill of Materials

Part	Finished Size* T	W	L	Mat.	Qty.
A* streets	1 1/16"	1 1/4"	10"	M	2
B center strip	3/4"	2 5/8"	10"	W	1
C* door	5/16"	2 13/16"	8 1/8"	W	1
D* doorstop	5/16"	2 13/16"	1 7/8"	W	1

*Parts marked with an * are cut larger initially, and then trimmed to finished size. Please read the instructions before cutting.

Material Key: M–Maple, W–Walnut
Supplies: Spray adhesive, finish.

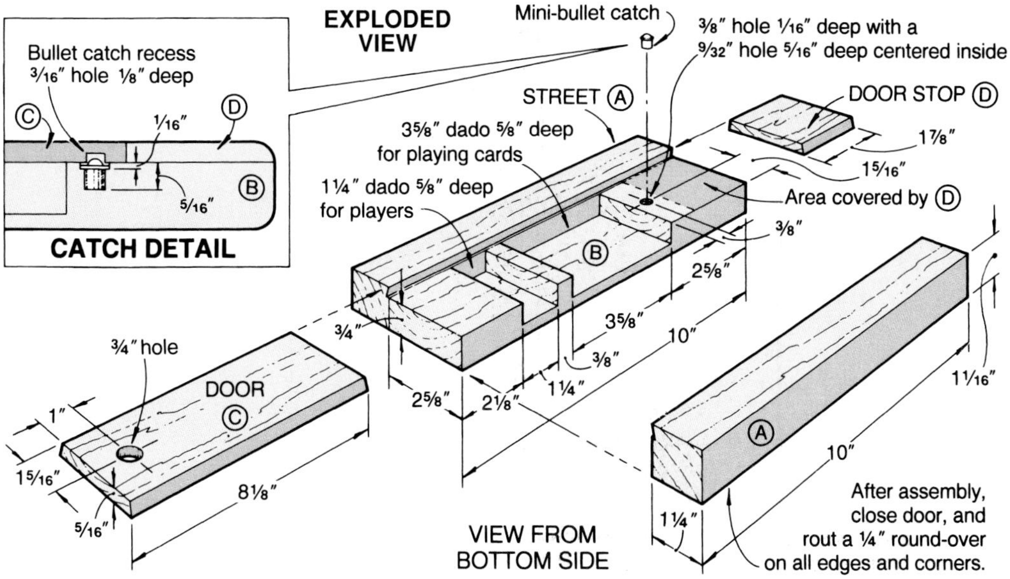
EXPLODED VIEW
Bullet catch recess 3/16″ hole 1/8″ deep
Ⓒ
Ⓓ
1/16″
5/16″
Ⓑ
CATCH DETAIL
Mini-bullet catch
3/8″ hole 1/16″ deep with a 9/32″ hole 5/16″ deep centered inside
STREET Ⓐ
3 5/8″ dado 5/8″ deep for playing cards
1 1/4″ dado 5/8″ deep for players
DOOR STOP Ⓓ
1 7/8″
1 5/16″
Area covered by Ⓓ
3/8″
2 5/8″
3 5/8″
3/8″
10″
3/4″
2 5/8″
2 1/8″
1 1/4″
3/4″ hole
DOOR Ⓒ
1″
1 5/16″
5/16″
8 1/8″
1 1/16″
Ⓐ
10″
1 1/4″
VIEW FROM BOTTOM SIDE
After assembly, close door, and rout a 1/4″ round-over on all edges and corners.

THE CONNOISSEUR'S CRIBBAGE BOARD
continued

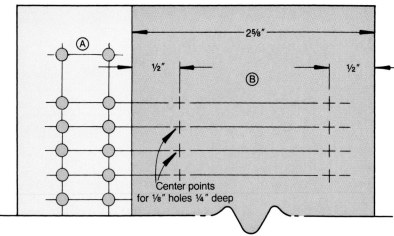

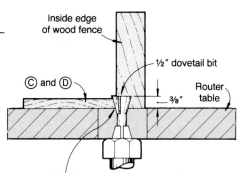

ROUTING THE DOOR AND DOOR-STOP STRIP

Inside edge of wood fence

½" dovetail bit

Ⓒ and Ⓓ

Router table

⅜"

Raise the router bit and realign the inside edge of the fence with the new intersection of the bit and router table.

2⅝"

½"

½"

Ⓐ

Ⓑ

Center points for ⅛" holes ¼" deep

3. With the bottom surfaces and ends flush, glue and clamp the center strip between the maple streets. Wipe off the glue squeeze-out immediately with a damp rag. Let the glue dry and then remove the clamps.

4. Mark the location, and drill the eight holes for the game score tracks where shown on the drawing *above*.

Make the door and door stop

1. Reposition the dovetail bit and router table fence where shown on the drawing *top right*. Rout along both edges of one of the ⁵⁄₁₆" walnut strips where shown on the drawing. Check the fit of the test strip between the dovetail grooves in the laminated board. If the thin strip is too wide, sand or plane one edge slightly, and rerout the edge until the piece slides easily.

2. Cut the door (C) and door stop (D) to length from the 12"-long piece.

3. With the ends flush, glue the doorstop to the center strip.

4. Backing the stock with scrap to prevent chip-out, drill a ¾"finger hole through the door where dimensioned on the Exploded View drawing.

Install the bullet catch

1. Press the bullet catch into the hole in the center walnut strip.

2. To locate the bullet catch recess in the door, slide the door open and shut several times. Remove the door, and drill a ³⁄₁₆" hole ⅛" deep at the end of the indented line scribed by the bullet catch. See the Bullet Catch detail.

Finishing up

1. Slide the door in place, and sand the cribbage board smooth. Now, rout a ¼" round-over along all edges and corners. With the door in place, sand cribbage board smooth.

2. Apply the finish. (For an even finish, we pounded nails through a scrap of wood where shown in the drawing *above right*. Then, we positioned the cribbage board upside down on the nails and sprayed on the finish. After the finish dried, we turned the board over, and sprayed the top of the board. To prevent the playing holes from clogging, we used an aerosol finish.) Apply paraffin to the edges of the dovetailed lid for a smooth slide. Finally, read 'em and weep.

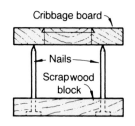

Cribbage board

Nails

Scrap wood block

Buying Guide

• **Cribbage board kit.** 10 black-, 10 red-, and 10 natural-colored wood players, 5 mini-bullet catches (enough for 5 boards). Stock No. 7672. For current prices, contact Meisel Hardware Specialties, P.O. Box 70, Mound, MN 55364-0700, or call 800-441-9870.

Project Tool List

Tablesaw
   Dado blade or dado set
Router
   Router table
   Bits: ½" dovetail, ¼" round-over
Drill press
   Bits: ⅛", ³⁄₁₆", ⁵⁄₃₂", ⅜", ¾"
Finishing sander

Note: *We built the project using the tools listed. You may be able to substitute other tools or equipment for listed items you don't have. Additional common hand tools and clamps may be required to complete the project.*

HAND-CARVED COOKIE MOLDS

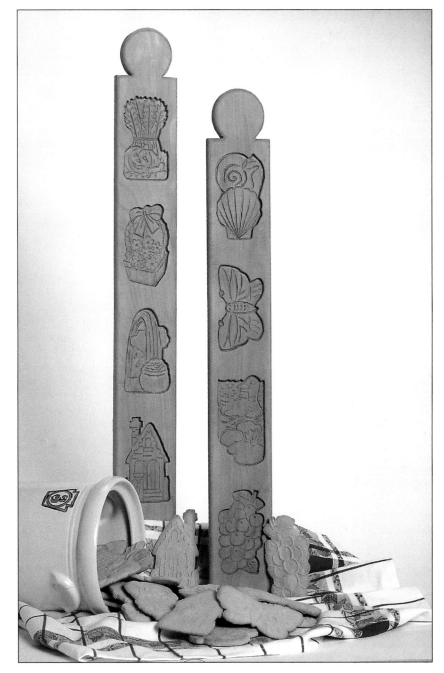

When you're ready for milk and cookies after doing this carving, you won't have to wonder where to get the cookies. Simply make them in your hand-carved molds using our *Better Homes and Gardens®* Test Kitchen recipe on *page 84.* Then, hang the molds on your kitchen wall for an old-time accent.

Cookies from woodcarvings

Woodcarvers and bakers first teamed up to turn out fancy cookies more than 400 years ago. From the mid-1600s until well into the 19th century, vendors at European fairs and markets hawked gingerbread portrayals of saints, royalty, and other popular figures.

Bakers accumulated a jumble of molds as they added new patterns. To cut down kitchen clutter, they would have several patterns carved on one board, sometimes on both sides.

Colonists brought the tradition to the New World, carving wooden molds with American themes. Machine-carved wooden molds became common during the 19th century. Later, metal and plastic cookie molds replaced them. Today, collectors treasure those old wooden cookie molds.

Now, let's get cookin'

Start with a ¾x3½x27" piece of beech for a functional four-mold board, or select your favorite carving wood for a decorative version.

Mark the centerpoint for the decorative rounded top where shown on the Cookie Board drawing, on *page 84.* Adjust your compass to 1½" to lay out the circle, and then draw a straight line across the top where shown to form the shoulders. Cut the top profile with your bandsaw or scrollsaw. If you plan to use your cookie molds often, carve them on a 24" board and omit the round top. Why? Leaving straight ends on the board makes it easier to slap it against a countertop to pop the cookies loose.

Draw a line across the board 1¼" above the bottom edge. Now, select four of the patterns on *pages 85* and *87* and photocopy them.
continued

HAND-CARVED COOKIE MOLDS
continued

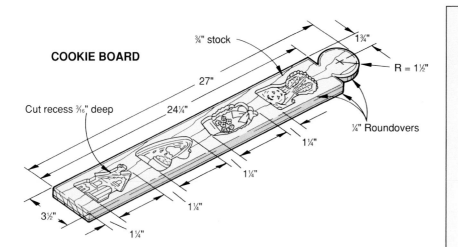

COOKIE BOARD

¾" stock

Cut recess ³⁄₁₆" deep

27"

24¼"

1¾"

R = 1½"

¼" Roundovers

1¼"

1¼"

1¼"

3½"

1¼"

With scissors or an X-acto knife, cut out each pattern, leaving a straight line across the bottom.

Pick the pattern you want for the bottom, and then lay it on the board with a piece of graphite transfer paper underneath. Align the bottom pattern edge with the line on the board, and center it from side to side.

Secure with masking tape, and trace the *red* outline onto the stock. A French curve and a straightedge will help you trace more accurately.

Next, draw a line 1¼" above the top of the pattern. Align the next pattern on that line. Repeat for a total of four designs on the board. After tracing the patterns, set them aside; you'll need them again later.

Carve out some reliefs

Treat each mold as a small relief carving. First, remove wood to a depth of about ³⁄₁₆" within the pattern outline to create the relief area, a process called *grounding*.

Start grounding with a vertical knife cut along the pattern outline. This cut, a *stop cut,* enables you to clean out wood with your gouge right up to the edge of the relief area without chipping out wood beyond it.

You also can stop-cut with the V-tool, but be sure to keep the

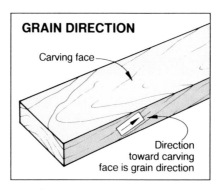

GRAIN DIRECTION

Carving face

Direction toward carving face is grain direction

cutting edge vertical. You'll need to stop-cut several times as you carve down to the final relief depth with your gouges.

You'll accomplish most of the grounding with ⅛" and ⁵⁄₁₆" No. 5 gouges. Although a ⁵⁄₁₆" No. 3 or 5 spoon gouge and a ⅛" No. 12 bent V-tool will come in handy, they aren't essential. Work down to depth in stages of stop-cutting and gouging out wood.

Work with the grain when cutting lengthwise. Our beech boards chipped out readily when we turned against the grain. To determine the grain direction, look at the edge of the board. Then, starting at about the middle of the edge, trace with your finger along one of the grain lines. The direction you move your finger along the grain line to reach your carving

face is the grain direction. (See illustration, *above left.)*

Keep the sides of your reliefs vertical or slightly flared. Be sure not to undercut them. (If you do, the dough won't come out of the

FULL-SIZED PATTERNS

continued

HAND-CARVED COOKIE MOLDS
continued

mold in one piece.) Carve a crisp junction between the side of the relief area and the bottom.

Maintain uniform relief depth within each mold. Be sure to carve all molds the same depth, too. The cookie dough shapes will bake better if they pop out of the molds the same thickness.

For quicker grounding, rout the pattern outlines with a ⅛" straight bit in a plunge router. Work down to final depth in several passes. Change to a larger bit to clear the middle of the recess.

For the smoothest project flow, ground all four molds on the board first. Then, carve the detail lines for each design, completing one mold before moving to the next one.

Add detail to your molds

With the grounding done, cut out the paper patterns along the *red* outlines. Trim each one to fit into its carved recess. Then, with a same-sized piece of transfer paper, trace the *black* lines for carving.

Cut the design with your ³⁄₆₄" or ⅛" No. 11 U-veiner, as appropriate. The veiner leaves a round-bottomed groove, which we think looks better than a V-shape for this job. Go at least ⅛" deep; deeper cuts, we found, make better-looking cookies.

Switch to gouges to carve the crescent shapes (duck feathers, for example). Select a gouge of the correct sweep and width for each. (Don't worry if you don't have a lot of gouges; a few will provide enough variety. A ⅛" and a ³⁄₁₆" No. 5 and a ¼" No. 7 did the trick for us.)

Cut crescents the easy way

Carve each one in two steps. (See photos, *above right*.) First, lean the gouge away from you at a

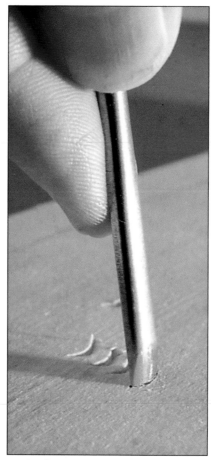

Begin the crescent with the gouge's bevel perpendicular to the carving surface.

slight angle so that the bevel on the back of the blade is perpendicular to the workpiece and facing you. Then, force it into the wood *(left-hand photo)*.

Next, with the gouge in the carving position, place a corner of the blade at one end of the curved incision and at a small angle in front of it. Now, roll the gouge around until the other blade corner meets with the opposite end of the arc *(right-hand photo)*.

Roll the gouge from one side of the arc to the other to complete the cut.

Finishing up

With the carving completed, rout a ¼" round-over along all edges and a hanging slot in the top center of the back side. Turn your ⁵⁄₁₆" No. 5 gouge over to complete the round-overs in the corners between the circle and the board.

Sand the board, rounding over the outer edge of each pattern recess. Finish with salad oil.

Project Tool List

Gouges: ⅛" No. 5, ¼" No. 7, ³⁄₁₆" No. 5 ⁵⁄₁₆" spoon gouge, No. 3 or 5 (optional)
V-tools: ⅛" No. 12, ⅛" No. 12 bent (optional)
U-veiners: ³⁄₆₄" No. 11, ⅛" No. 11
Knife: Bench-type carving knife

Note: *We built the project using the tools listed. You may be able to substitute other tools or equipment for listed items you don't have. Additional common hand tools and clamps may be required to complete the project.*

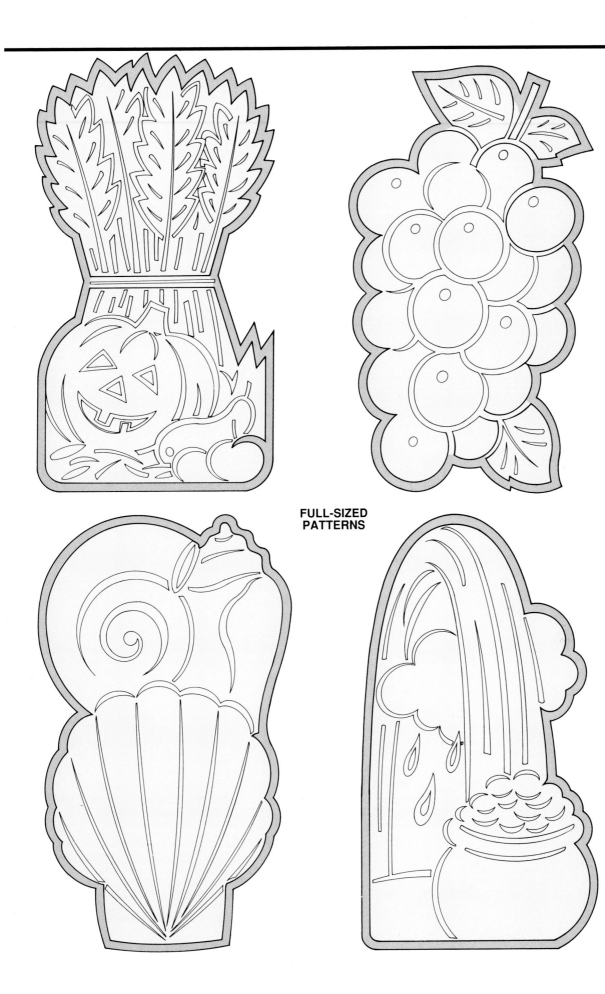

FULL-SIZED PATTERNS

A JEWELRY BOX OF A DIFFERENT STRIPE

Note: You'll need some thin stock for this project. You can resaw your own or order stock.

First, the case

1. Rip and crosscut enough ¼" stock to glue up the case top and bottom (A), sides (B), and back (C). Cut the pieces 1" longer and ¼" wider for trimming to finished size later. Lay out and match the pieces for the best grain pattern; then glue and clamp them as shown in the Edge-Joining drawing, *below.*

2. Scrape off the squeeze-out and sand the joints smooth. Trim the case top, bottom, and side pieces to finished size.

3. Use a tablesaw with a dado blade or a table-mounted router with a ¼" straight bit and fence to cut ¼" rabbets ⅛" deep on the back edge of the top and bottom panels (A). Use the same setup to cut the rabbets on the top, bottom, and back edges of the side panels (B).

4. Lay out and mark the position of the dadoes on the side panels (B) where indicated in the Exploded View drawing. Use a tablesaw and dado blade or a router table with a fence and a ¼" straight bit to cut ¼" dadoes ⅛" deep where marked on the side panels.

5. Cut the shelves (D) to size, then dry-fit the case assembly (A-B-D) together. Glue and clamp the case assembly, checking it for square.

6. When the glue has dried, carefully trim the back panel (C) to fit snugly into the case assembly. Glue the back panel in place. Remove the excess glue after it forms a tough skin.

7. Using a router fitted with a ¼" round-over bit, rout all exterior edges of the case *except* the top front edge. (Leaving the front edge square allows the drawer top to fit tightly against the case as shown in the Cutaway Side View drawing, *below.*)

Now for the drawers

1. To make the ½"-thick drawer fronts (E), cut six pieces of ¼" zebrawood to 2¼" wide by 10¼" long. Now, glue two pieces together for each drawer front in sandwich fashion, keeping the edges as flush as possible. You'll end up with three ½"-thick laminations.

EDGE-JOINING

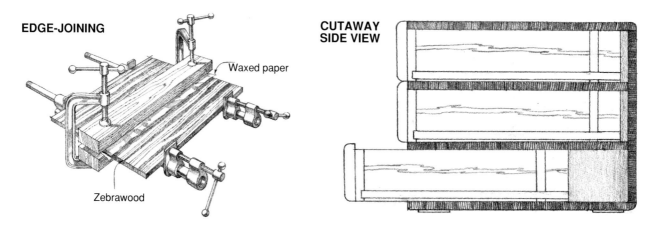

Waxed paper

Zebrawood

CUTAWAY SIDE VIEW

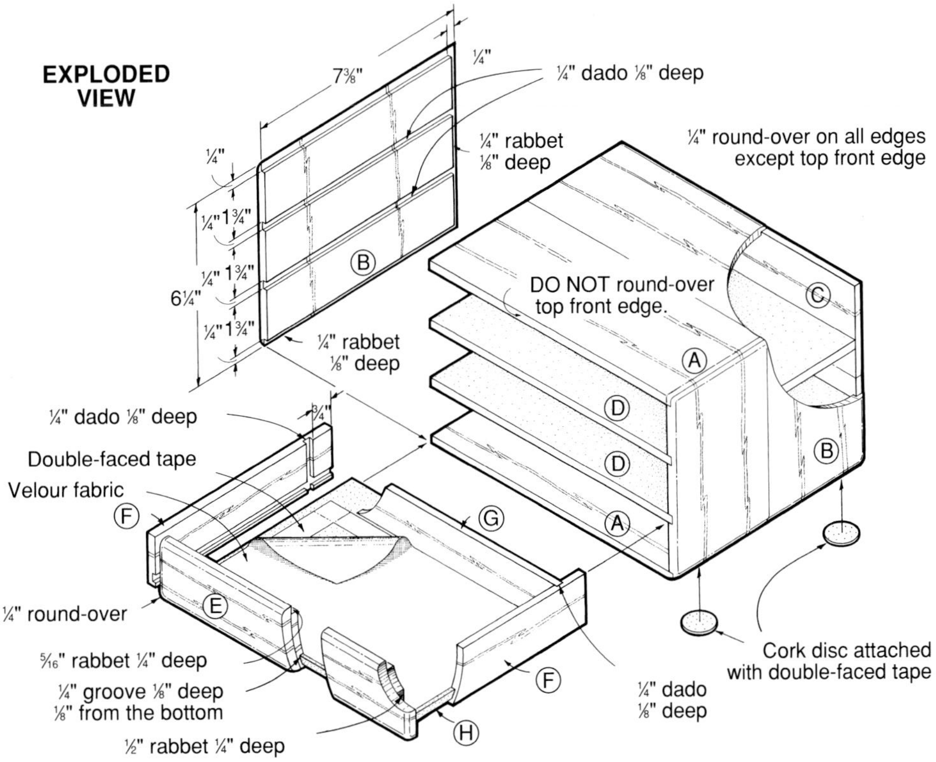

EXPLODED VIEW
7⅜"
¼"
¼" dado ⅛" deep
¼" rabbet ⅛" deep
¼" round-over on all edges except top front edge
¼"
¼" 1¾"
¼" 1¾"
6¼"
¼" 1¾"
B
DO NOT round-over top front edge.
C
¼" rabbet ⅛" deep
A
D
D
B
A
¼" dado ⅛" deep
¾"
Double-faced tape
Velour fabric
F
G
¼" round-over
E
5/16" rabbet ¼" deep
¼" groove ⅛" deep ⅛" from the bottom
F
¼" dado ⅛" deep
Cork disc attached with double-faced tape
½" rabbet ¼" deep
H

Part	Finished Size*			Mat.	Qty.
	T	W	L		
A*	¼"	7⅜"	9¾"	Z	2
B*	¼"	7⅜"	6¼"	Z	2
C*	¼"	6"	9¾"	Z	1
D	¼"	7⅛"	9¾"	H	2
E*	½"	2"	10"	Z	6
F	¼"	1 11/16"	7"	Z	6
G	¼"	1 5/16"	9 3/16"	Z	3
H	¼"	7"	9 3/16"	H	3

Bill of Materials

*Parts marked with an * are cut larger initially, and then trimmed to finished size. Please read the instructions before cutting.

Material Key: Z–zebrawood, H–hardboard
Supplies: Velour fabric, double-faced tape or spray-on adhesive, cork or felt, lacquer sanding sealer, clear gloss lacquer finish.

2. Rip and crosscut the three laminated drawer fronts (E) to finished size (2x10").

Note: *Because the drawers are identical in size, we constructed all three at the same time, making the cuts on all corresponding parts before changing our saw or router setup.*

3. Using your tablesaw or router, cut a ½" rabbet ¼" deep on both ends of the drawer fronts (E). Then, cut a 5/16" rabbet ¼" deep on the top edge of each. And, finally, use a router table with a ¼" round-over bit to shape all the outside edges of the fronts.

4. Cut the drawer sides (F), backs (G), and bottoms (H) to size. Cut a ¼" groove ⅛" deep and ⅛" up from the bottom edge of the fronts (E) and sides (F). Also cut a ¼" dado ⅛" deep; ¾" from the back of the drawer sides (F), as shown in the Exploded View drawing *above*.

5. Dry-fit the drawer assemblies (E-F-G-H) to ensure a good fit, then glue and clamp them together, checking for square.

Time to finish and admire

1. Fit the drawers into the case, sanding if necessary for a good fit. Finish-sand the case and drawers.

2. Apply two coats of clear lacquer sanding sealer followed by two coats of gloss lacquer. Don't forget to finish the inside of the box to minimize warpage. (*Tip*: After the last coat of lacquer had thoroughly dried on our jewelry case, we coated the bottom edge of the drawer sides [F] with paraffin wax to ensure smooth gliding.)

3. Cut the drawer liner fabric and cork foot pads to size and attach them with double-faced tape or spray-on adhesive. Felt would also work fine for the foot pads.

Project Tool List

Tablesaw
- Dado blade or dado set

Router
- Router table
- ¼" round-over bit

Finishing sander

Note: *We built the project using the tools listed. You may be able to substitute other tools or equipment for listed items you don't have. Additional common hand tools and clamps may be required to complete the project.*

TOP-DRAWER DESK SET

Customize your office or home desktop in style with this handsome trio of helpful accessories. We sandwiched thin layers of maple between pieces of walnut to create the snappy business look seen on all three projects.

Note: You'll need thin stock for this project. You can either resaw or plane thicker stock to the thicknesses listed in the Bill of Materials. Or, see our source of preplaned stock in the Buying Guide.

For starters, form the maple and walnut lamination

1. Cut two pieces of ½"-thick walnut and one piece of ½"-thick maple to 3⅞" wide by 48" long.

2. Apply a thin, even coat of woodworker's glue to the mating surfaces. With the edges and ends flush, glue and clamp the pieces face-to-face in the configuration shown in Step 1 of the five-step drawing *opposite.*

3. Remove the clamps from the lamination, scrape the glue from one edge, and joint or plane that edge flat. Now, rip the *opposite* edge for a 3¾" finished width.

4. Referring to Step 2 of the five-step drawing, center the blade on the lamination, and make two cuts where shown to resaw the lamination in two. (We used a thin-kerfed carbide-tipped blade.)

5. Joint or plane the ripped surface of the maple shown in Step 3 of the drawing. Decrease the thickness to ⅛". If doing this on a jointer, use a push block for uniform pressure and to keep your fingers safely away from the cutters. Repeat for the second piece of laminated walnut and maple.

6. Crosscut the two 48"-long laminated pieces in half. Then, cut a piece of ½" walnut to 3¾×24". Glue and clamp the five pieces face-to-face with the edges and ends flush in the configuration shown in Step 4 of the drawing.

7. Scrape the glue from one edge. Then, joint or plane the scraped edge flat.

8. Using the dimensions in Step 5 of the drawing, place the planed edge against the tablesaw fence, and rip one ⁵⁄₁₆"-thick piece and five ⁷⁄₁₆"-thick pieces from the laminated block.

9. Lightly plane or sand both surfaces of each laminated strip to remove the saw marks and reduce the thickness of the ⁷⁄₁₆" strips to ⅜" and the ⁵⁄₁₆" strip to ½".

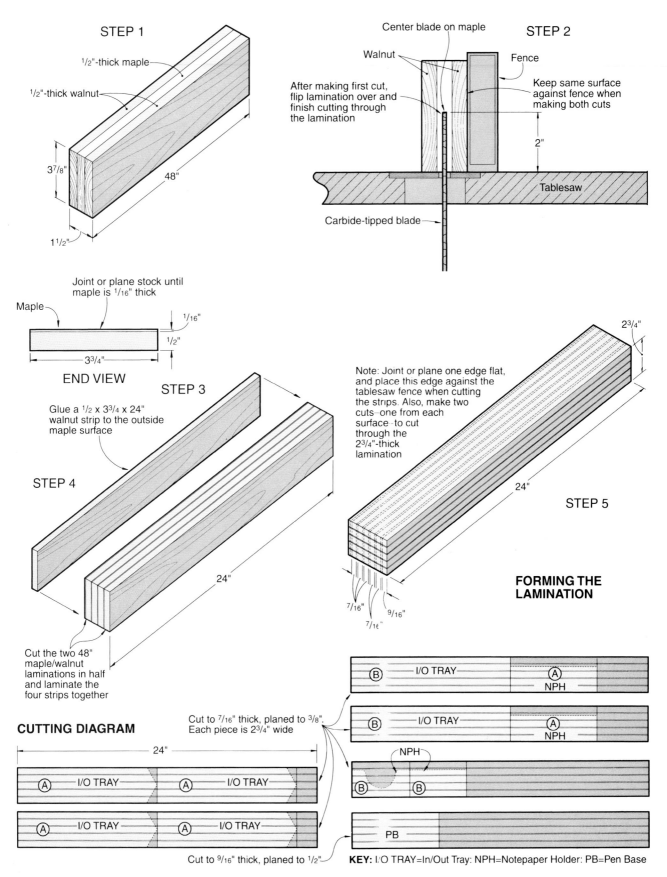

STEP 1

$^1/_2$"-thick maple

$^1/_2$"-thick walnut

$3^7/_8$"

48"

$1^1/_2$"

STEP 2

Center blade on maple

Walnut

Fence

After making first cut, flip lamination over and finish cutting through the lamination

Keep same surface against fence when making both cuts

2"

Tablesaw

Carbide-tipped blade

Joint or plane stock until maple is $^1/_{16}$" thick

Maple

$^1/_{16}$"

$^1/_2$"

$3^3/_4$"

END VIEW

STEP 3

Glue a $^1/_2$ x $3^3/_4$ x 24" walnut strip to the outside maple surface

STEP 4

24"

Cut the two 48" maple/walnut laminations in half and laminate the four strips together

Note: Joint or plane one edge flat, and place this edge against the tablesaw fence when cutting the strips. Also, make two cuts—one from each surface—to cut through the $2^3/_4$"-thick lamination

$2^3/_4$"

24"

STEP 5

FORMING THE LAMINATION

$^7/_{16}$"

$^9/_{16}$"

$^7/_{16}$"

CUTTING DIAGRAM

Cut to $^7/_{16}$" thick, planed to $^3/_8$". Each piece is $2^3/_4$" wide

24"

| Ⓐ | I/O TRAY | Ⓐ | I/O TRAY |

| Ⓐ | I/O TRAY | Ⓐ | I/O TRAY |

Cut to $^9/_{16}$" thick, planed to $^1/_2$"

| Ⓑ | I/O TRAY | Ⓐ | |
| | | NPH | |

| Ⓑ | I/O TRAY | Ⓐ | |
| | | NPH | |

NPH

| Ⓑ | Ⓑ | | |

| | PB | | |

KEY: I/O TRAY=In/Out Tray: NPH=Notepaper Holder: PB=Pen Base

continued

TOP-DRAWER DESK SET

continued

Bill of Materials				
Part	**Finished Size**		**Mat.**	**Qty.**
	T	**W**	**L**	
NOTEPAPER HOLDER					
A sides	⅜"	2³⁄₁₆"	7"	WM	2
B front & back	⅜"	2³⁄₁₆"	4⅝"	WM	2
C bottom	¼"	4½"	6½"	WP	1
IN/OUT TRAYS (2 TRAYS)					
D sides	⅜"	2¾"	11⁵⁄₁₆"	WM	4
E backs	⅜"	2¾"	12⅞"	WM	2
F fronts	⅜"	2⅛"	12⅞"	W	2
G bottoms	¼"	9¹³⁄₁₆"	12¾"	WP	2
H connectors	½"	1¾"	8"	W	2

Material Key: WM–Laminated walnut and maple, WP–walnut plywood, W–walnut, **Supplies:** clear finish, rubber or felt self-adhesive feet.

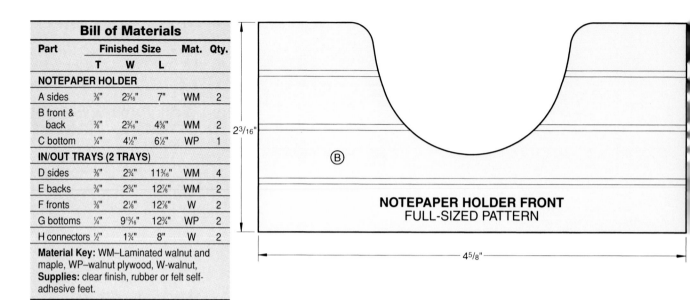

NOTEPAPER HOLDER FRONT
FULL-SIZED PATTERN

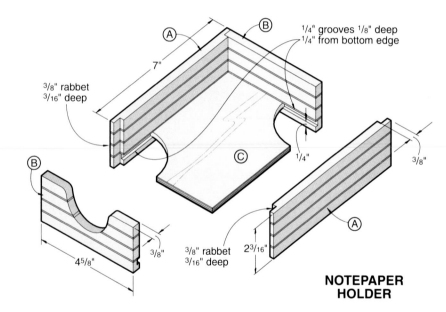

¼" grooves ⅛" deep
¼" from bottom edge

⅜" rabbet
³⁄₁₆" deep

7"

⅜" rabbet
³⁄₁₆" deep

3/8"

4⅝"

2³⁄₁₆"

3/8"

NOTEPAPER HOLDER

Cut and assemble the notepaper holder

Note: *Our holder is designed to house 4×6" notepaper, available at most stationery stores.*

1. Cut the notepaper holder sides (A) and front and back (B) to the sizes listed in the Bill of Materials.

2. Cut a ⅜" rabbet ³⁄₁₆" deep across both ends of the side pieces where shown on the Notepaper Holder drawing. Then, cut a ¼" groove ⅛"

deep, ¼" from the bottom inside edge of all four pieces.

3. Transfer the full-sized front view pattern to the front piece (B). Bandsaw the piece to shape, and then sand the cut edge smooth to remove the saw marks.

4. From ¼" plywood, cut the bottom (C) to size. (We used walnut plywood; you also could choose a less-expensive plywood and stain the top exposed face with a walnut stain.)

5. Dry-clamp (no glue) the pieces to check the fit; trim if necessary. Sand the pieces smooth. Glue and clamp the notepaper holder together, checking for square.

6. Sand a slight round-over on all edges with 150-grit sandpaper.

Next, construct the in/out trays

Note: *The instructions are for two trays and a pair of connectors.*

1. Crosscut four side pieces (D) and two back pieces (E) from the laminated stock to the sizes listed in the Bill of Materials.

2. Cut a ¼" groove ⅛" deep and ¼" from the bottom edge in each side and back piece where shown on the In/Out Tray drawing.

3. Using the drawing titled Cutting the Miters *opposite* for reference, miter-cut the front end of each side piece.

4. Switch to a dado blade, and readjust the stopblock location on your miter-gauge auxiliary fence. Then, using the drawing titled Cutting the Rabbets for reference, cut a rabbet along the bottom front edge of each side piece as shown in the photo *opposite*.

5. Adjust the miter gauge square to the blade, reposition the stopblock, and cut a ⅜" rabbet ³⁄₁₆"

CONNECTOR DETAIL

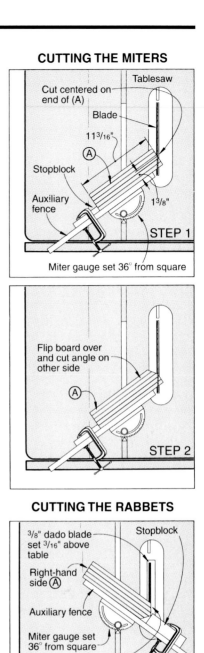

CUTTING THE MITERS

Tablesaw

Cut centered on end of (A)

Blade

11³/₁₆"

(A)

Stopblock

Auxiliary fence

1³/₈"

STEP 1

Miter gauge set 36° from square

Flip board over and cut angle on other side

(A)

STEP 2

IN / OUT TRAY

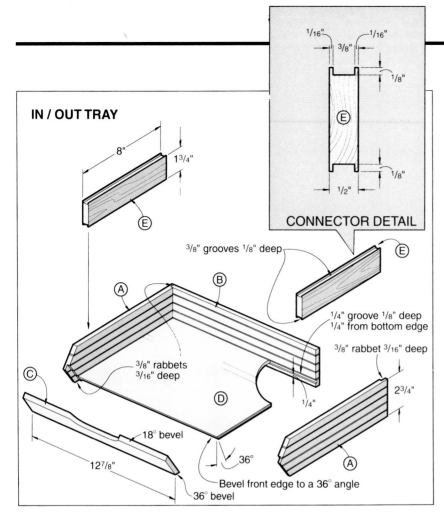

8"

1³/₄"

(E)

³/₈" grooves ¹/₈" deep

(B)

(E)

(A)

¹/₄" groove ¹/₈" deep
¹/₄" from bottom edge

³/₈" rabbet ³/₁₆" deep

³/₈" rabbets
³/₁₆" deep

(C)

(D)

2³/₄"

¹/₄"

(A)

18° bevel

12⁷/₈"

36°

Bevel front edge to a 36° angle

36° bevel

CUTTING THE RABBETS

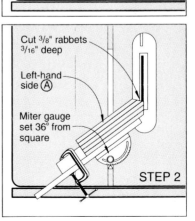

³/₈" dado blade set ³/₁₆" above table

Stopblock

Right-hand side (A)

Auxiliary fence

Miter gauge set 36° from square

Cut ³/₈" rabbets ³/₁₆" deep

STEP 1

Cut ³/₈" rabbets ³/₁₆" deep

Left-hand side (A)

Miter gauge set 36° from square

STEP 2

Using a miter gauge and a dado blade mounted to your tablesaw, cut a rabbet along the bottom front edge of each tray side piece.

continued

TOP-DRAWER DESK SET
continued

deep along the back inside edge of each side piece.

6. From ⅜" walnut (solid stock), cut the tray fronts (F) to size. Transfer the full-sized tray front half-pattern to the inside face of the tray fronts. You'll need to do this twice on each front to transfer the entire pattern.

7. Bevel-rip the top and bottom edges of the front pieces (F) to the angles stated on the Tray Front End View pattern.

8. Bandsaw, and then sand the opening in each walnut tray front (F) to shape.

9. Cut the plywood tray bottom (G) to size, bevel-ripping the front edge where shown on the In/Out Tray drawing.

10. Dry-clamp each tray to check the fit, and trim if necessary. Sand the pieces smooth. Glue and clamp

each tray together, checking for square.

Add a pair of connectors

1. To make the trays stackable, cut two connectors (H) to size from ½"-thick walnut.

2. Using the dimensions on the Connector detail accompanying the In/Out Tray drawing on the *previous page*, cut a ⅜" groove ⅛" deep centered along both edges of each connector.

3. Check the fit of the connectors on the mating pieces of the tray sides (D). The fit should be snug to prevent wobble. Sand the connectors smooth.

Make a simple pen holder

1. Crosscut the laminated pen holder base to 7" long from the ½"-thick lamination.

2. There are numerous pen sets on the market. (We selected a set where the funnels come with self-adhesive bottoms; other available funnels screw to the wood base.) See the Buying Guide for our source, or select your own. Sand the pen base.

Add the finish, and attach the pen funnels

1. Finish-sand the notepaper holder, in/out trays, connectors, and the pen base. (Using a sanding block, we started with 100-grit, and proceeded to 150-grit, and finally 220-grit sandpaper.) Sand a slight round-over along all edges, especially along the curved front opening of the in/out tray and notepaper holder.

2. Adhere the funnels to the base where shown on the drawing

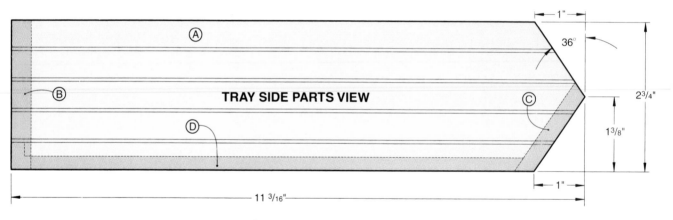

TRAY SIDE PARTS VIEW

FRONT VIEW (FULL-SIZED PATTERN)

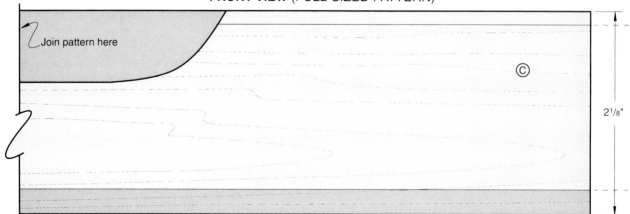

Join pattern here

at *right*. (We found that the funnels stick better if you apply them before applying the finish. See the Buying Guide for our source of the pen, pencil, and funnels.)

3. Mask the pen funnels, and apply the finish to all the parts. (We applied several coats of Deft spray lacquer finish, steel wooling lightly between coats with 0000 steel wool. Since off-the-shelf steel wool is often protected from rust with a light coat of oil, we rinsed our steel wool beforehand with lacquer thinner to remove any oil. The oil from uncleaned steel wool can transfer to the wood and contaminate the finish. Also, rub lightly to prevent buffing through the finish to the bare wood.)

4. Apply self-adhesive rubber, cork, or felt pads to the bottom of the pen holder. Remove the masking from the pen funnels.

Buying Guide
•**Executive pen and pencil set.** Gold-colored pen, pencil, two funnels, and two self-adhesive bases. Kit No. WM1292-B. For current prices, contact Cherry Tree Toys, P.O. Box 369, Belmont, OH 43718, or call 800-848-4363.

PEN HOLDER

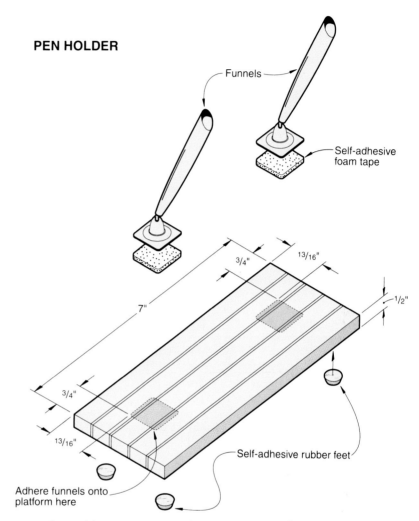

Funnels

Self-adhesive foam tape

3/4"   13/16"

7"   1/2"

3/4"

13/16"

Self-adhesive rubber feet

Adhere funnels onto platform here

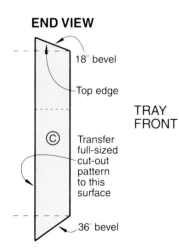

END VIEW

18° bevel

Top edge

Ⓒ Transfer full-sized cut-out pattern to this surface

36° bevel

TRAY FRONT

•**Hardwood kit.** Five pieces of ½x3¾x24" walnut, four pieces of ⅟₁₆x3¾x24" maple, plus stock cut slightly oversize for notepad holder part C and tray parts C, D, and E. All-sanded surfaces (no knife marks). Stock No. W1292. For current prices, contact Heritage Building Specialties, 205 North Cascade, Fergus Falls, MN 56537, or call 800-524-4184.

Project Tool List
Tablesaw
   Dado blade or dado set
Jointer
Bandsaw
Finishing sander

Note: *We built the project using the tools listed. You may be able to substitute other tools or equipment for listed items you don't have. Additional common hand tools and clamps may be required to complete the project.*

ACKNOWLEDGMENTS

Project Designers

Nancy Armstrong—Top-Drawer Desk Set, pages 90–95

Don Bailey—Bud Vases with Flair!, pages 55–56

Kat Beals—Hark the Herald Critters Sing!, pages 5–7

Karen and August Caryl—One Whale of Notepad Holder, pages 60–61

Pat Darcy with Joy, Inc.—Holiday Candle Holder, pages 30–31

Sandy Decker and Marilyn Kriegshauser—Deck the Halls, pages 22–23

James R. Downing—Seasonal Silhouettes, pages 11–13; Hardwood Bookends, pages 58–59; The Three Rack-A-Tiers, pages 62–63; The End-Grain Cutting Board, pages 64–65; The connoisseur's Cribbage Board, pages 80–82; A Jewelry Box of a Different Stripe, pages 88–89

Kim Downing—Hark, the Herald Critters Sing, pages 5–7

George Egan—Rockabye Doll Cradle, pages 71–75

C.L. Gatzke—Chimney-Topped Candle Holder, page 57

Sarah Grant-Hutchison—Away in a Manger, page 40–53

Mary Lou Hanson—Twelve Scrollsawed Days of Christmas, pages 14–16

Alan Hoyt—Christmas Tree Ornaments, pages 38–39

Hank Laub—Jingle Bells Sleigh, pages 24–27

Ronald L. Mackey—Carve a Holiday Angel, page 8; Chip-Carved Snowman, pages 34–37

Daryl Morgan—Jewel of a Case, page 67

Keith Raivo Designs—Handwoven What-Not Basket, pages 76–79

Jim Stevenson—Hand-Carved Cookie Molds, pages 83–87

Fern Weber—Carved NOEL, pages 32–33

Chuck and Julie Wiemann—Colorful Christmas Blocks, pages 28–29

Donna Wood—Sweet-Tooth Santa, pages 17–21

Photographers

Bob Calmer
David Haas
John Hetherington
Hopkins Associates
William Hopkins
Jim Kascoutas
Scott Little
Perry Struse

Illustrators

Jamie Downing
Kim Downing
Randall Foshee
Mike Henry
Lippisch Design Inc.
Carson Ode
Chuck Stearns
Jim Stevenson
Bill Zaun

If you would like to order any additional copies of our books, call 1-800-678-2802 or check with your local bookstore.
